Help!

What is My Purpose?

Understanding Life Purpose and
How to Discover Yours

By
ADA ANISIOBI

Published by 50Dot7 LLC, California.

Disclaimer: This is a work of nonfiction. It is not intended to provide personalized professional advice. Readers are encouraged to seek the counsel of competent professionals with regards to such matters. Neither the author nor the publisher shall be liable for any loss or damage incurred.

Many of the characters and events are fictitious and a product of the author's imagination. For some that are not, their identity has been altered to preserve confidentiality.

ISBN: 979-8-9871360-0-3

For further information and business enquiries, please email: info@50Dot7.com

Dedication

Mr. Josiah & Mrs. Joy Anisiobi.

Seasoned educators, insightful leaders and loving parents. Your keen eyes observed the unique potentials of my siblings and I. You guided and supported us in our journey to develop them and pursue our purpose. Raising seven children through the university is not a walk in the park.

Thank you very much, I love you.

Acknowledgements

I am deeply grateful for the mentorship of Dr Sunday Adelaja, Kyiv, Ukraine whose inspiration enabled me to harness certain untapped potentials within me.

To Katerina Koronis, I appreciate you for all your assistance. And to my friends and siblings who would prod me on, thank you!

Table of Contents

Introduction

It's well known that teenage and early adult years are periods marked by confusion and frustration, as the adult child attempts to discover their identity as a fully-fledged adult. Many questions arise during this time. Who am I? Why am I here? What do I become? What career should I pursue? What should I do with my life?

At some point, we must figure out what to do with our lives. There are several ways to arrive at a decision and most are wrong. Once a wrong path is chosen, it leads to a wrong destination. Some young adults' paths are mapped out by parents or peers, while some find no path, so they merely drift. Drifting can lead to wrong choices and a lot of frustration.

I understand because I've been there. As a teen, I was so confused it was pitiful. Recently, I was reminded of my anguish after reading some comments on social media. I heard young people crying for help, guidance and direction. One girl wrote, "Please help me, I don't know what to do with my life."

I was moved to provide a solution. I had the answer they were seeking. And I knew I had to help before they wasted their lives. This book is that answer.

The real problem isn't ignorance of the right career but ignorance of purpose – life purpose. Most young people haven't heard about life purpose, much less how to discover it. They, as well as many adults, don't realize that there is a definite reason for their lives.

Help! What is My Purpose? was written to teach people, especially young adults, the meaning of life purpose since it is fundamental to their identity as humans. It also explains the consequences of ignorance of life purpose. Most importantly, it explains how to discover their purpose since seven chapters are dedicated to the discovery of purpose.

Furthermore, *Help! What is My Purpose?* shows the readers how to select a career based on their purpose. By matching several purpose clues, the readers can arrive at the career they were created for. And finally *Help! what is my Purpose* teaches the readers what to do next, having discovered their purpose for living.

This book is a must read for any young adult who is confused and grappling to find their path in life. It is also a must read for adults who are not on their destiny path. It will redirect and empower them to live a purpose-centered life.

Help! What is My Purpose? is a part of my *Preparation for Life* series. This is a series of books that contain information that will equip young adults for starting life on their own.

Part 1

What is Life Purpose?

Chapter 1

What is Life Purpose?

"A person without a purpose is like a ship without a rudder." —Thomas Carlyle, Scottish Historian and Philosopher

"Help!" she cried. "I don't know what to do with my life!"

This was a passionate plea from a young university graduate. She had spent four years in university, paid huge sums of money for tuition, yet she was clueless as to her path, now she had finished studying.

Have you ever wondered what you're supposed to do with your life? Have you ever experienced confusion regarding your direction? Or have you experienced an overwhelming feeling of emptiness in your current job or pursuits, groping for something to fill the void, yet you have no clue what it is?

These are signs that you're seeking your life purpose or your calling.

Life is defined as the period from birth to death of a living thing, while purpose is defined as the reason something exists or is done, an intended or desired result. Therefore, life purpose can be defined as the reason for the existence of an individual human being. It is the intended or desired result for the period from birth to death of a person.

Your life purpose therefore is the result you're expected to produce during your life, between your birth and your death. This result is pre-determined, so you don't choose it; rather, you discover what it is. So, my question is: do you know what this result is?

Let's do a simple exercise here. What is the purpose of your cell phone? What is the purpose of your car? What is the purpose of your house? Easy? Now, the big one, what is the purpose of your life?

It's interesting to know that many people have never considered this last question before, while some who dared came up short, because they couldn't figure out the answer. Life purpose attempts to answer the questions, "Who am I?" "Why am I here?" and "What am I here to do?"

Live for Purpose

"It's not enough to have lived. We should be determined to live for something."
—Winston S. Churchill

Unfortunately, most people go through their lives merely existing. They don't live for something; they don't identify and live their purpose. There's widespread evidence to prove that, beginning with the jobs they do. Many are working just to fulfill financial obligations and keep the bill collectors away.

They work because they have to, not because they love to. That's why the acronym TGIF (Thank God It's Friday) is immensely popular. Many workers are glad on Fridays when they can take a break from their detestable jobs.

While they love Fridays, the feeling is the opposite for Mondays. The following Mondays memes, though hilarious, truly represent widespread feelings people experience about their work.

"What's that stench? Oh... it's Monday!" "Monday...not again!" "Not sure if I hate Mondays or Mondays hate me." "Why is Monday so far from Friday and Friday so near to Monday?" "I hate Mondays!" (1)

Oh, yes, a lot of employees worldwide hate Mondays because they hate their jobs. Gallup, a Washington DC-based organization, has been monitoring the level of employee satisfaction worldwide for decades and their reports are quite revealing. According to their 2021 Gallup World Pool, 20% of employees feel engaged at their jobs. (2)

This means that a staggering 80% of employees worldwide are not engaged at work. Some of them feel no sense of passion or deep connection to their job, while others outright hate their job. Some employees sleepwalk through the day, putting minimal effort into their tasks. For these 80% of employees, work is more often a source of frustration than satisfaction!

These are global figures!

Besides the negative impact on productivity, more alarming are the consequences for the overall health and well-being of these employees. The ensuing debilitating stress, which is capable of ruining one's health, could manifest as headaches, muscle aches, irritability, changes in appetite and anxiety. Further buildup of the stress hormone cortisol could lead to worsening symptoms in mood, mental health, and blood pressure.

These negative health consequences may trickle into relationships, creating tensions in homes and aggravated behaviors towards loved ones and, in extreme cases, can result in physical violence or suicide. In Japan, where the employee dissatisfaction figure is as high as 94%, the ensuing stress, clinical burnout and subsequent suicide rates are so alarming, they actually have a term for death caused by overwork or job-related exhaustion: Karoshi.

All because of one's job!

But work is supposed to be a positive activity that provides goods, services, and income. How did something inherently good become a source of such frustration to a staggering 80% of the world's employees? Why is work a source of stress, burnouts, physical and emotional problems for humanity?

The answer is that many people are working against or outside of their life purpose. They participate in activities they were neither created nor designed to do. Let's consider this analogy.

A young chicken sees a bird flying in the sky. She is captivated. "I want to fly, I want to fly!" she gushes. Then she compares herself to the bird and observes they both have wings, feathers, and legs. So, she decides that henceforth she would rather fly than walk.

Imagine the stress, strain and aches this chicken would experience at the end of the day, after flying for eight hours. Now, extrapolate it for the next five or ten years!

Most employees could be likened to this chicken that chose to fly like a bird. Although we humans resemble each other in a lot of surface ways, we are designed differently within our beings. And the majority haven't discovered their unique design and what they were designed to do. Therefore, they do the wrong jobs.

These 80% haven't discovered their life's purpose – that which they were created and designed to do.

Your purpose is what makes you unique, and it determines what you should do with your life. Although the chicken resembles the bird doesn't mean it should fly. In the same vein, having a brain, arms and legs doesn't mean you should do just any work. You must find out your innate design to avoid falling into the 80% category.

Now, let's talk about the 20% who are engaged at work. These are the few who have discovered their life purpose. They love their job, not necessarily because they have the best working conditions, bosses, or colleagues, but because they are doing what they were created to do. They don't experience burnout for working 40 plus hour weeks; rather, they feel rejuvenated and fulfilled. Don't you want that for yourself?

The Peanut Man, George Washington Carver, was a professor of Agriculture at Tuskegee University, Alabama, USA. He was renowned for his research on peanuts, which led to the development of over three hundred products, including paper, cosmetics, soaps, and oils.

The story was told how Carver went into his laboratory on a Monday morning and was not seen again for days.

By Friday, his concerned colleagues broke down his door, only to see Carver busy with his experiments. The irritated Carver complained about their rude interruption, arguing that it was only noon. He was surprised to learn that, although it was noon, it was noon on Friday! He was certainly in the 20% category!

Confucius, an ancient sage who lived about 479 BC, explains it clearly: *"Choose a job you love, and you will never have to work a day in your life."*

The right job ought to energize, inspire and fulfill you. It should be fun, enjoyable and awaken your curiosity and creativity. If your job drains you, stresses you out and leaves you exhausted, then you're working outside of your life purpose. You exist for a reason, you're alive for a reason. You were genetically designed to perform a specific task and that task is your purpose.

Our Earth is an orderly planet. Everything has its purpose, for example, the trees, flowers, rivers, etc. Unfortunately, humans are the only creatures that have a challenging time understanding that they, too, have a unique purpose on Earth.

If you are confused about what your purpose is, then you're reading the right book. Personally, I was confused for many years. At some point, I was begging everyone in my family to tell me what course to read at university. Even after graduation, I couldn't settle with a career path.

Since I struggled a lot in this area, it has become my passion (and purpose!) to help others who face similar challenges. There are many materials out there that emphasize how important it is to pursue your purpose, but they don't tell you how to know what your purpose is. This only worsened my frustration. "Could someone just tell me how?" I'd complain.

I've put this book together to address that problem. I want to teach you the importance of purpose and, more importantly, show you step by step how to discover yours and select a career based on your purpose.

This book is divided into two sections. The first section deals with the subject matter, purpose, while the second section lists practical ways to discover your purpose. Some of you may discover your purpose in the first section but I encourage you to read till the end.

I also encourage you to share what you learn with friends and family members who are struggling in this area, especially the young ones. My passion is to save young people the stress of living a life outside of their purpose.

This isn't a Guidance and Counselling book. So, teens, please don't hide it under the couch or bury it beneath a pile of dirty laundry. How I wish I'd received this book in my teenage years. It would have spared me a lot of trouble!

Now, with that said, let's dive in and explore this subject called purpose. What is life purpose?

Chapter 2

Purpose is Your Earthly Chore

"The secret of success is constancy to purpose."
—Benjamin Disraeli

Every human being has a chore on Earth. You may have been born into a family where you didn't perform household chores, yet you're not exempt from this one. It's the reason for your existence on Earth. And your contribution to justify the free oxygen the Earth gives you. Purpose is that chore, task, or assignment you were created to fulfill.

Whether you were born with a silver spoon in your mouth or into the most impoverished family, you've got an earthly chore to do. Being wealthy doesn't exempt you. So long as you're alive and well, you're expected to add value to the world, using the talents and abilities within you.

One erroneous belief is that work is purely for making a living or paying bills. This belief is held especially by the 80%, who view their work only as a means of fulfilling financial obligations. It is also seen among some wealthy people, who assume that being rich has absolved them of their need to work. So, they laze around and contribute nothing to the society.

Everyone is born with a purpose, regardless of their family's financial status. And life expects you to use your talents to fulfill your purpose and make the world a better place. Your purpose is your work. And your purpose is not for financial fulfillment, but for the betterment of others.

Therefore, a person born into a wealthy family could use their painting abilities to produce artworks that will inspire people. They could use their eloquence or natural charisma to promote a cause to help certain groups of people in society. But to claim an exemption from purpose because one's financial needs are met is a misuse of life.

Similarly, poverty doesn't exempt one from serving humanity. You must discover your purpose and pursue it. In the process, you will not only serve humanity, but you will also attain financial fulfillment.

Purpose is the Problem You Were Created to Solve

For some people, their life purpose is found in the problems they were born to solve. Our world has certainly got a lot of problems. We face problems such as hunger, poverty, global warming, human trafficking, terrorism, opioid crises, and suicide. In addition to existing problems, new ones emerge all the time, such as Ebola, Zika and Coronavirus (COVID -19.

Imagine a world where no one is pursuing solutions to these problems – it would be completely uninhabitable. Fortunately, some people are created to seek solutions to these problems. While some search for cures in laboratories, others advocate for new laws and reforms, while some create awareness and generate resources. As a result, our world isn't overwhelmed with problems.

Mully is a movie about Dr. Charles Mully, a self-made millionaire in Nairobi, Kenya, who gave up his comfort to provide a home to thousands of homeless children, living on the streets of Kenya.

Dr. Mully himself was homeless for years, having been abandoned by his family. As a teenager, begging on the streets, Mully almost committed suicide. Fortunately, he experienced a turnaround when he got a job. He went on to become a self-made millionaire, enjoying a life of luxury with his wife and eight children.

However, Mully couldn't forget the plight of homeless children roaming the streets, begging for food. He knew he had to tackle that problem. So, he gave up his comfortable life and opened his doors to them. He did not just feed them, they lived in his house, clothed, and cared for.

Eventually, his house was not big enough, so Mully moved to the suburbs and onto a large piece of property, where he built houses and a school for these children. They had grown to number thousands! They grew their own food and had their own school.

As a result of this arrangement, Dr Mully has been able to transform the lives of over fifteen thousand homeless kids, who are now doctors, lawyers, entrepreneurs and so on, living in various parts of the world. Mully Children's Family (MCF) is the largest children's rehabilitation organization in Africa.

Dr Mully's life purpose is solving the problem of homelessness for young children. You too should discover the problem you were created to solve and actively tackle it. So long as everyone is busy solving one problem or another, our world will keep getting better.

Mully didn't just improve the lives of homeless children, he also improved the level of security in his society, by channeling those kids away from a life of crime.

Purpose is Your Work, Not Your Job

"A lot of people quit looking for work as soon as they find a job." —Zig Ziglar

Your purpose is the work you are expected to do on Earth. According to New York bestselling author, Myles Munroe, a job is what you do till you discover your work, and your work is your purpose.

A job is an activity you do in exchange for money. But working at a job doesn't mean that you're doing what you were created to do. So, let's define a job as non-purpose activities, and work as your purpose. This means a lot of us, especially the 80% category, are simply doing a job, while the 20% have discovered their work.

Sometimes, on the path of preparation for their purpose, people engage in diverse types of job to earn money or gain knowledge. That's okay if they understand that it's temporary and just a means to an end. But to spend one's life doing a job that satisfies financial obligations but has no connection to your purpose is a misuse of your life.

At some point in my life, I took a highly paid job in an industry I had no business being in. I was a pharmacist working in the telecoms industry. Don't ask if I was dispensing medications because I wasn't working in a clinic! Anyway, it was temporary because I was simultaneously pursuing a postgraduate degree in pharmacy.

I was often amazed that I was well paid, yet I was only using a tip of the iceberg per my potentials. As a result, I was bored! That's what happens when people are in the wrong jobs. There is no demand on their innate potential and creativity and, as a result, they become bored and irritated and hop from one job to another.

But while on this job, I became keenly aware of my true passions. I was often nominated to attend training courses and thereafter train my colleagues. It was only when I stood up as an instructor, training my colleagues, that I experienced some joy. I knew then, without any doubt, that I was created to impart knowledge.

I want you to understand what purpose truly is and be able to differentiate it from just any job. That someone is performing a task, providing goods or services, doesn't mean they were created to do so. Although I was working and providing services, I wasn't working in my purpose. All I had was a job, not my real work. Purpose is your real work!

Purpose is Your Service to Humanity

"True happiness... is not attained through self-gratification, but through fidelity to a worthy purpose." —Helen Keller

A particularly important characteristic of purpose is that it's not self-centered. So, when you think about purpose, you should ask, "How can this make my society, country or the world a better place?" But if your thoughts are, "How can this meet my financial needs?" then it has failed the purpose test. You were created to serve humanity. So, your purpose must align with this important criterion.

Let's look at Emeka, for instance. He was a senior executive in a commercial bank in the city. He had built a distinguished career for himself, climbing through the ranks. His wife, family and close friends were immensely proud of his achievements, so they organized a huge party to celebrate his most recent promotion. Although his colleagues admired and envied his position, Emeka often felt a sense of emptiness.

He didn't understand why the emptiness prevailed. He had what he'd always wanted. He'd worked hard and made a lot of sacrifices, yet it felt so empty now that he'd achieved it.

He couldn't confide in anyone because he felt stupid – how would he explain his frustration, when others around him would gladly trade places with him?

During a time of reflection, Emeka realized that, although he was particularly good at his job, he experienced the greatest sense of accomplishment while mentoring junior colleagues. He decided to assess his assumptions and developed a system to train junior workers on the success principles that had helped him climb the corporate ladder.

Suddenly, Emeka came alive. He enjoyed his classes, and the awed students were excited to learn from the boss. Later, Emeka started a non-profit organization to educate young, entry-level, and junior executives about success secrets in the workplace. As he explained to his wife and close friends, the joy he feels when he sees the erstwhile timid young people metamorphose into confident high achievers is unquantifiable.

Emeka discovered the purpose of living – joy and fulfillment in life is tied to serving humanity, not in accumulating wealth. As Albert Einstein said, "Only a life lived for others is a life worthwhile." We must discover our purpose in life because it's only when we're actively working on it that we experience the joy and contentment of life. Are you like Emeka, highly accomplished yet experiencing a deep emptiness that you cannot explain? Then it's time to find out exactly what your life purpose is.

Purpose is Serving Others with Your Gifts

"Where your talent and the needs of the world cross, lies your calling." —Aristotle.

Purpose is your legacy. It's your service to humankind in the area of your talents and gifts. According to the Greek philosopher Aristotle, your calling (purpose is using your gifts or talents to solve the problems of humanity. You're fulfilling your purpose when you're serving humanity with your gifts and talents.

Your gifts and talents were deposited in you for the purpose of serving others. But many don't use their talents to make the world a better place. Many merely use their time and energy to provide goods or services, while relegating their unique talents to the background. Most of these people are the 80% of employees we discussed earlier.

For instance, Hugo is talented musically. He's what I call musically intelligent (more on different types of intelligence later). However, Hugo works as a store manager in a local retail store. Although Hugo is providing services for humanity, he isn't fulfilling his purpose. He is not serving humanity with his unique talents and giftings.

As a result, Hugo will not experience that sense of fulfillment that comes through fulfilling one's purpose. That emptiness will prevail. Hugo is also prone to burnout and stress because he's doing what he was neither created nor designed to do. Renowned psychologist Abraham Maslow expresses it succinctly.

"Musicians must make music, artists must paint, poets must write if they are ultimately to be at peace with themselves. What humans can be, they must be."

Are you naturally eloquent and articulate? Are you a gifted dancer, designer, entertainer, teacher, beautician, or writer? Are you serving your community, or the world with these gifts, in exchange for financial remuneration, or are you simply exchanging your time and energy for money?

During the Covid-19 pandemic, we saw health professionals who risked their lives to save others. Many lost their lives in the process, yet no one could have persuaded them to abandon the sick because of the risks involved. They served humanity, despite the risk. Life purpose is about serving others and making the lives of others better.

"I slept and dreamt that life was joy,

I woke and saw that life was service,

I acted and behold, service was joy."

—Rabindranath Tagore
(Bengali poet of Kolkata)

Life isn't merely satisfying when you serve humanity with your gift and talents, it's rewarding, too.

There are consequences for every action. Scientists say it in a smart scientific way - action and reaction are equal and opposite (Newton's third law). This suggests that there must be consequences for living without a proper knowledge of one's purpose. Come with me as we explore some of these outcomes.

The Golden Nuggets

- ➢ Purpose is your earthly chore, task, or assignment.
- ➢ Every human being, irrespective of financial status, has an earthly chore.
- ➢ This chore falls into three categories – providing goods, services or solving problems.
- ➢ Purpose is the problem you were created to solve to make the world a better place.
- ➢ Purpose is not your job, it's your work.
- ➢ Purpose is not about you, it's about humanity – making life better for humans and animals, too.
- ➢ Your purpose is your contribution to the world.

Study Exercises

- What is life purpose?
- What are the broad categories of our assignment on Earth?
- What are the problems of life that bother you?
- What types of goods or services would you like to provide to others?
- Do you have a job right now? Is it your purpose or just to pay the bills?
- Purpose is not about you but about whom? Why?
- Can you think of people whose jobs are not their work? How can you tell?
- Can you describe instances where you think someone is working in their purpose? Why do you think so?
- What are the huge rewards of working in your purpose?

Chapter 3

Consequences of Ignorance of Purpose

"When the purpose of a thing is unknown, abuse is inevitable." —Dr Myles Munroe

Since abuse is inevitable when purpose is unknown, according to late New York Times bestselling author and speaker, Dr Myles Munroe, then we may conclude that many people abuse or misuse their lives, due to ignorance of its purpose.

The impact of ignorance of purpose transcends low productivity at work and stress-related health issues. We experience it in our communities and our nations, although we may not have attributed it to ignorance of purpose. However, the following outcomes could be traced to ignorance of life purpose because they represent an abuse or misuse of life.

Crime

Criminal activities, such as robberies, prostitution, drugs, human trafficking, and gang-related activities, depict ignorance of one's purpose. Life purpose isn't about doing the right work but understanding that your life should make the world better. Crime doesn't improve the world, so it's contrary to purpose.

Interestingly, there have been dramatic changes in criminals after they discovered their purpose. One of such is Curtis Carrol, a young man serving a life sentence in San Quentin prison, USA.

Curtis was born into a life of crimes and at age 17, he was convicted of murder. While in prison, he realized that his life could become meaningful and have a positive impact on others. He learnt how to read and write and went on to learn about the stock market.

Popularly known as "Wall Street," Curtis has become a highly respected and sought-after stock market expert and advisor. He also runs a financial literacy and investment program that educates inmates and prison staff about the stock market. Instead of a life of crimes, Curtis is teaching financial literacy behind the four walls of a prison.

Teen Pregnancy

Some years ago, I saw several teenagers become pregnant immediately after high school. It was shocking because I'd interacted with their parents and assumed they were headed on the right path. Although they were smart young girls, it dawned on me that they had no inkling of their life purpose.

A deep understanding and appreciation of their purpose could have protected these girls from such costly mistakes. That's why every parent must understand this and pass the message to their children. Purpose will give a young girl the vision, focus and fortitude to resist momentary pleasures that afterwards create a life of pain and regrets.

Suicide

While I was in pharmacy school, we learnt of a brilliant teenager from a poor family, who'd just gained admission to study pharmacy. Not only was she the oldest child, but she was also her family's hope for a better future. Unknown to her parents, Cathy was dating her physics teacher. One day, during a Valentine celebration, she visited and found him with an older lady. She was so devastated that she came home and committed suicide, destroying not only her own life but also the hopes of her loved ones.

Many young girls are traveling this horrible path these days and it's heart-breaking. This is ignorance of life purpose in action. An understanding of life purpose creates a deep appreciation for the gift of life. You're alive to impact your society and make the world a better place. Therefore, one ought to treat life as a precious jewel and concentrate on making the best out of it.

In addition, knowledge of her purpose would have given Cathy a deep sense of value and self-worth. Although it hurts to have your heart broken, rationally, how many girls end up marrying their first love? Many have to kiss several frogs before meeting their Prince Charming!

Your life is a special gift, designed to complete an important assignment on Earth. So, resist any temptation to end your life, no matter how compelling. Please open up to the people around you and get all the help you can. Don't end your life because our world needs you!

Suicide rates are on the increase, especially in developed countries. In the US, according to the National Institute of Mental Health, suicide is the second highest leading cause of death for individuals between the ages of 10 and 34.[3] In 2016 alone, suicide was responsible for over 45,000 deaths in the US. Among teens, research has attributed most of these suicide deaths to bullying.

I heard an incredibly sad story of a twelve-year-old, who was bullied by his classmates because he was different. He loved certain hobbies that were deemed 'old school.' He loved hunting, old-fashioned clothes and old music. He was repeatedly told to kill himself and eventually he succumbed, throwing his loving family into anguish.

I was deeply moved because this clearly depicts a lack of understanding of purpose. The ignorant bullies failed to realize that the boy was unique because of his purpose. As we will learn later in the book, your uniqueness is a clue to discovering your purpose in life. It's possible that this boy could have blended a mix of the old and contemporary, thereby creating new products, either in music, art, or fashion. Unfortunately, we'll never know because those potential products are buried with him. So sad!

Laziness and Complacency

Having been privileged to live in both the developing and developed worlds, I have found out that a lack of understanding of purpose breeds laziness and unproductivity in both worlds. While those in developing countries bemoan the unavailability of jobs, the ones in the developed countries bemoan the unavailability of government benefits and stipends.

Young people desperate for jobs often shut their minds to ideas and inspiration that could make them successful, if channeled towards their life purpose. A life of purpose, however, will inspire you to create opportunities for yourself and for others. And instead of waiting for the government, you'll be creating jobs.

One young lady faced the widespread problem of unemployment after graduating from the university. After years of futile job searching, she decided to look within and pursue her life purpose. She loved shoes so she started buying and selling shoes to friends and people around her.

As her business grew, an opportunity arose. Someone asked her, "Would you like to learn how to make your own shoes?" She agreed, did the training, and became a shoemaker. Today, she not only makes shoes, but she also trains and employs shoemakers.

Knowledge of life purpose will cause you to look inwards, discover why you were created and propel you to pursue it, irrespective of the availability of jobs. There are many people whose purpose has nothing to do with a corporate job, but ignorance of their purpose leaves them whining and complaining about the unavailability of government jobs.

In the developed world, I have seen young people who are complacent and demotivated, because they have no idea what to do with their lives. Although they have great tertiary institutions and lots of incentives, such as scholarships and grants, they are more interested in government handouts.

What wasted lives and wasted opportunities! Meanwhile, our world is waiting for young people everywhere to unleash the greatness within them and make the world a better place. How I wish they'll get a hold of this book and discover what to do with their lives!

Ignorance of purpose is a universal problem that produces the same results everywhere. It has no respect for age, race, gender, or nationality. The rich and the poor, celebrities, and nonentities, all feel the biting effects of not knowing their life purpose. Therefore, it's crucial for everyone to understand their life purpose and accomplish it.

Let's look at some of the benefits of understanding your purpose.

Benefits of Understanding Life Purpose

The benefits of a deep understanding of your life purpose cannot be over-emphasized. Its numerous advantages are clear in our individual lives and our societies. As we've already discussed, knowledge of life purpose gives you access to the privileged 20%, who are enjoying their work without stress. In addition, the following are some of the advantages of knowing your life purpose.

Improved Self-Worth

One of man's greatest needs is a sense of worth and importance. And a lot of young people are consumed with this need. To satisfy it, some indulge in destructive activities and lifestyles, ranging from crime, drugs, prostitution, gangs and so on. However, your life purpose will confer on you a sense of identity and worth.

Your life purpose also gives you a sense of belonging, a sense of importance and value. As a result, it protects you from the need to join certain circles, in order to be 'cool' or important. You're important because you have a purpose to accomplish.

Vision

Purpose produces vision. It gives you an inner picture of what you could be and do. It gives you a mental image of a world of possibilities. As a result, you are inspired, motivated, focused and goal oriented. Because your purpose has created a known destination, you're inspired to become disciplined.

This could mean saying no to the wrong friends, activities or habits that would deter you. Knowing your purpose and vision for life will enable you create boundaries that will prevent anyone or anything from taking advantage of you.

A Sense of Responsibility

I heard a popular TV personality tell the story of a man who was incarcerated for many years in the US. When he came out of prison, he was determined to live differently. He couldn't get an office job because, in addition to his criminal history, he was uneducated. So, he got a job mowing lawns.

After a year or two, he had saved enough money to buy his mowing equipment and began his own business. He still couldn't read or write but he was proud of his achievements. He announced to all who cared to listen that he was a business owner. Some years later, he proudly announced that he owned a house, a Mercedes, a Cadillac, and a Jacuzzi!

The beauty of this story is that it shows how purpose can change your perspective about life. There are a thousand and one reasons why this former felon could have reverted to a life of crime. But purpose made him realize he could add value to humanity, by mowing lawns and beautifying the neighborhood. And when he traveled the path of purpose, he was rewarded with the finer things in life, whether he could write them or not!

Fulfillment and Joy

Life feels empty when you're living outside your purpose. Your purpose is like a huge void within you, yearning to be filled. Money, fame, or power cannot fill that void, only your purpose can. Knowing and working in your purpose brings a completeness and fulfillment that makes life satisfying.

Now, let's get to that question that has been nagging at you for a long time. We shall discover the answer in a moment. Ready? Let's do it!

The Golden Nuggets

➢ Ignorance of life purpose is a major reason most people are doing the wrong jobs.

➢ Ignorance of life purpose runs across all age brackets, economic backgrounds, and nationalities.

➢ Most of the problems in our society, like crimes, suicide, and teen pregnancy, can be traced back to ignorance of life purpose.

➢ A good understanding of purpose equips one with vision, focus and inner strength.

➢ Fulfillment comes in the course of pursuing one's purpose.

Study Exercises

➢ Are there signs or manifestations of ignorance of purpose in your life?

➢ How did you arrive at your current job, career, or college course? Was it an offshoot of your parents' suggestions, friends or out of the blues?

➢ Do you feel empty, despite the remuneration and accolades that come with your job?

➢ Is there a yearning to be more, do more and impact more lives positively with your abilities?

Chapter 4

Born to Accomplish Purpose

"All of us are born for a reason, but all of us don't discover why. Success in life has nothing to do with what you gain or accomplish for yourself. It's what you do for others."
—Danny Thomas, founder of St Jude Children's Research Hospital.

W hy were you born?

"I don't know, I guess my parents wanted kids."

"I was a mistake. My parents were not married."

"My mum was raped. I wasn't supposed to be here."

"I was picked up beside a trash bin."

Regardless of your answer, one thing is certain; you were born for a reason. You may have arrived here through unconventional means, but there is a reason for your existence. That's because there is a reason for everything created on Earth.

Born for a Reason

I want to repeat this so it will sink in. You were born for a reason and you're here on a mission. You're not a mistake, even if your parents or the rest of the world think so. And you're important and unique, because you were created differently from every other person, living or dead.

You're so unique that no living or dead person shares the same DNA make-up as you. In fact, your DNA sequence is so unique that there are more than three million variations between yours and any other person's. Now, doesn't this make you feel special? It sure makes me feel good about myself!

In addition, you should feel more special because, out of the seven billion people on the planet today, no one has the same fingerprints as you. No one ever has and no one ever will share your fingerprints. Now, that's another good example of uniqueness! Therefore, despite the stories surrounding your birth, you must realize that you're unique, specially created, and different from everyone else, and there is a reason for all that.

Surely there must be a reason you won the race in your mother's womb! Scientists tell us that, during fertilization of the female egg or ovum, millions of sperm are released but only one wins the race and that's you. You're not one in a million but one in several million!

"Oh, spare me, that's just a coincidence," you may argue. "After all, one sperm was always going to win the so-called race!"

Yes, one sperm was going to win but, coincidentally, it happened to be you! So, celebrate your existence. It does not matter if you were picked up beside a trash bin, just get excited because you're about to discover through the pages of this book, the reason you're here.

In 1953, a young man in the small town of Kosciusko, Mississippi, USA, saw a teenage girl. She was wearing a poodle skirt and his curiosity was aroused. He wanted to know what was under the skirt and she obliged him. That casual act under an oak tree got her pregnant. And the baby girl?

She was unwanted, unplanned for, a terrible mistake. But she grew up to become a successful talk show host, actor, media executive, philanthropist, billionaire, and sometime richest Black woman in the world! Her name is Oprah Winfrey. Do you still think that your pathway into this world matters?

You were born for a reason – to fulfill a purpose. This is what makes your life special. So, despite your birth circumstances, your goal is to discover what your life purpose is. And you have taken the right step by reading this book. Let's proceed to discover why you won that special race in your mother's womb!

Designed for Purpose

It is important to understand that you weren't just created for a reason, you were also designed for a reason. You were designed with certain strengths, abilities, and talents that make it easy to fulfill your life purpose. I know that many young people wish they looked different, who doesn't! Many would love to exchange their body for someone else's. They want A's face, B's personality, C's hourglass figure, while envying D for his six-pack!

But I have good news for you today. You were created in harmony with your life purpose. Your looks, physique, intelligence, temperament, aptitudes were all designed to match your life purpose. So, stop wishing you looked like another person; their design may not be suitable for your assignment. If you were supposed to be an athlete, it may not benefit you to look like a size zero model; that physique may not withstand rigorous exercises.

Some people are designed to manage more mental work, while some are designed to handle more physical work. Whichever category you fall into, understand that your physical design points to your life purpose. Everything that is created in nature is designed with regards to its purpose. When you see a creature with fins, you instinctively know that it's meant to swim. And a creature with legs tells you that it's designed to walk. So, when you look at your unique traits, they are clues as to what your purpose is.

A mom told the story of her three teenagers, who'd read a book on how to achieve success and implemented it in separate ways. The younger ones were diligent and academically smart, but the oldest was a high school drop-out, who was more interested in body-building exercises. According to the mom, he was also the outcast of the family and caused her a lot of worries.

The middle child wanted to go to college but, since her parents couldn't afford it, she got a job and, by implementing the ideas from the book, she was quickly promoted to a managerial position. She started making enough money to enroll into college. The youngest followed his sister's footsteps, became successful and enrolled in college, too.

The oldest saw the progress of his younger siblings and was challenged. He wanted to make money, but he was not brilliant; moreover, he had played truant for too long. After reading the book, he realized that he was designed differently from his siblings and his passion was different, too. So, he got a job as a bouncer. He looked the part and did his work so passionately that he was recruited to become a part of the Presidential security team.

This young man realized he was designed in harmony with his purpose. He did not give up on himself because he was not academically inclined like his siblings. He discovered his purpose through his passion and physique and became successful. So, don't let anyone make you feel bad about your design; instead, discover why you were so designed, then pursue and fulfill that purpose. Realize that every person is designed in accordance with their life purpose.

No Purpose is Superior to Another

Now, let's discuss another important fact about purpose. No life purpose is superior to any other. This means that your purpose isn't better than mine, nor mine better than yours. Just like our body parts are all important and none is superior to another, so also is life purpose.

Every part has a unique function. The heart cannot walk, so why should it feel more important than the legs? Although the appendix has no known function, the pain of an inflamed one can reduce a grown man to tears. Maybe it exists to humble us, or what do you think?

On a more serious note, no life purpose is superior to any other. Therefore, you should not be intimidated by another person's purpose. For example, a pilot isn't superior to a chef. Sure, he can fly planes, but he may not prepare a delicious plate like the chef. And the world needs both the pilot and the chef. The goal is for everyone to be good at their purpose because, ultimately, we're all here to serve one another and make the world a better place.

So, don't despise yourself if your purpose is to be a cleaner and don't let another diss you because theirs is to be an aeronautical engineer. So long as you do what you were designed for and you're serving humanity, you're fulfilling your life purpose. Donna was also a janitor, and her story will interest you.

Donna's story is a good illustration that no purpose is superior to any other. You can become successful in your purpose, even if it isn't a 'top-notch' or 'reputable' profession. Donna was cleaning people's homes, even though she had a college degree in Sociology. She had a passion to make places look clean and neat – her life purpose.

As demand for her services increased, she hired more hands to help her. Eventually, she set up her janitorial business, Team Clean Inc. and, fifteen years later, it was the largest female-owned business in the city of Philadelphia, USA. According to the company's website, Team Inc. boasts over seven hundred employees. As a result of her achievements, Donna L. Allie has been decorated with numerous awards.

Her story is proof positive that, even if your purpose is to be a janitor, you can turn it into a success. You're serving humanity by providing clean homes and office spaces. And in return, life rewards you with financial gains and fulfillment.

The problem isn't with your life purpose but with the individual. Some reject their purpose because others despise them. As a result, they are not inspired with ideas to turn it into huge enterprises like Donna did. But once you reorient your mindset, regard your life purpose as important and allow yourself to be inspired, you'll be amazed at what you'll achieve. This is because no life purpose is superior or inferior to others.

Purpose Brings Riches and Fulfillment

"Oh, but an aeronautical engineer earns more than a chef," One may argue. This question raises a particularly crucial point regarding life purpose. Purpose isn't overly concerned about financial rewards. I know you want to make money – we all do, but the longer you live, the more you'll realize that fulfillment hardly comes from money.

Now, that's not a suggestion that money isn't important, far from it. Money is good; it solves a lot of problems and makes the world merrier. Despite that, you must never sacrifice life purpose on the altar of riches. The proper thing is to discover your life purpose, then seek to become successful at it. And as you achieve success, money follows naturally.

Ralph Waldo Emerson, the famous American philosopher and poet, said, *"It is one of the most beautiful compensations in life... we can never help another without helping ourselves."*

So, don't put the cart before the horse. Don't seek a career because it's more lucrative; instead, find out what you were created to do and become the best at it. Then, you'll be financially rewarded.

Get Paid for What You Love!

> *"Find out what you like doing best and get someone to pay you for it."*
> — Katherine Whitehorn, British journalist

The reason you should pursue purpose is that it brings both riches and fulfillment. Both are encapsulated within your life purpose. Your purpose is the place where you'll shine effortlessly because it's your area of strength.

It's also the place where people will pay you for doing what you love.

A popular footballer explained that he loves football and would play it willingly for free. However, it never ceases to amaze him that people will pay him to do what he loves! That is a life of purpose.

Most people's definition of work is doing something they dislike, just to earn money. But purpose is doing something you love and getting paid for it. Steve Jobs, co-founder of Apple Computers, said, "The only way to do great work is to love what you do." Working your purpose will bring so much joy and satisfaction that it will not feel like work. If everyone discovered their life purpose, there would be less stress and burnout and great motivation in the workplace.

No millionaire or billionaire ever became rich, doing what they hated. Employees are usually the ones who hate what they do but keep doing it. How about you discovering your purpose and letting the world pay you for it?

And that's exactly what we're going to do! I'm so excited for you, I can hardly wait for you to join me in the second part of this book where you get to practically unravel your life purpose. Ready, let's plunge in!

Golden Nuggets

➢ Your purpose is the reason you were born.

➢ The circumstances surrounding your birth do not diminish your worth.

➢ You were physically and mentally designed to match your life purpose.

➢ No purpose is superior or inferior to any other.

➢ Each person's purpose is supposed to create a better life for humanity.

➢ Riches, success, and fulfillment are encapsulated within your purpose.

Study Exercises

➢ Does every human have a life purpose?

➢ What makes you special and important?

➢ Do family and birth circumstances determine who has a life purpose?

➢ What are your peculiar designs that may be related to your life purpose?

➢ Are there inferior and superior life purpose?

➢ What is the right attitude towards one's purpose?

➢ How can one turn an 'inferior' life purpose into a terrific opportunity?

➢ What is your idea of work? Are you right or wrong based on what you've learnt?

➢ Would you set a goal to discover your purpose and enjoy getting paid for it? If your answer is yes, then turn the page, so I can show you how!

Part 2

How to Discover Your Life Purpose

Part 2

How to Discover Your Life Purpose

Welcome to the second part of this book. Being here means you said yes to my last question! I hope you're enjoying the journey so far. You've learnt a lot about life purpose. This knowledge is not available to many – so congratulate yourself for acquiring it. However, we're going to take this journey a step further.

Now you understand what life purpose or calling is, you're going to discover yours. Some of you may have discovered yours from the snippets I shared in the previous section. But in this section, we're going to be more practical, and I would advise you to do the following:

- ➢ Grab your journal and a pencil.
- ➢ Respond to every question I ask.
- ➢ Write down thoughts and ideas that flip across your mind as you read.
- ➢ Don't over-think your answers.
- ➢ Answer the study questions at the end of each chapter.

Something that bears repeating: Don't overthink your answers, just write down all the thoughts that pop up in your mind. You'll go back and edit them before you get to the last chapter. The important thing in the first instance is to give your mind free rein to present any and every thought and idea that might come to you.

Now, the first thing to know about your life purpose is that your purpose is already within you.

Your Purpose is Within You

This sounds so simple, yet it's a major puzzle to those attempting to discover their life purpose or calling. Some people look externally to discover their purpose. They seek answers from other people, their environment, family heritage or societal trends.

Some become entrepreneurs because their family has a history of entrepreneurship. Some choose law because their parents are attorneys, or they suggested it. Some observe popular trends such as IT and join the bandwagon, like I did. But your purpose is hidden right within you!

Since your purpose is within, you must study yourself. Place yourself under a magnifying glass and analyze yourself. That's how to discover your life purpose. So, let's get to it. We've placed you under the microscope and the first thing we're going to look at is your passions – the things you love.

Chapter 5

What do you Love?

"We lose ourselves in the things we love. We find ourselves there, too." —Kristin Martz

I was at a furniture store the other day and I struck up a conversation with a young sales assistant named Diego. I asked if he had discovered his life's purpose. He responded in the affirmative and I couldn't help but ask, "What is it?"

"A mortician," he replied.

The flower vase almost fell from my hands.

"A mortician?" I repeated, to confirm I heard him correctly.

"Yeah," he responded.

Now I was intrigued. This was strange and, from his strikingly handsome and gentle features, I'd never have guessed this purpose.

"How did you arrive at that?" I asked.

Diego replied that he loves quiet, and corpses are so quiet, they attract him. He went on to explain that he hates noise but feels an extraordinarily strong appeal in the quietness around corpses.

Wow, I was amazed. I could tell he had discovered his life purpose through his passion - his love for quiet and tranquility. Your life purpose is not a mystery. It isn't difficult to discover, either. It's within you and there are hints that reveal what it is. The first clue to your purpose is that it's something you love and enjoy.

Perhaps you've heard that your purpose might be something you absolutely dislike or detest.

For instance, you dread talking to strangers and you agonize that your purpose may be public speaking, marketing or a profession that connects you to strangers. No, that's incorrect! I want to restore your peace of mind. Your purpose isn't something you dread or dislike; rather, it's something you love with a passion!

You were born to do something you love, not something you dislike. Something you enjoy, that you're enthusiastic about. That's because, when you're doing what you love, you become energized and motivated. You get infused with an inner strength. The enthusiasm and strength from within keep you going when difficulties arise.

In addition, your purpose is hidden in the things you love, because when you're engaged, there's a flow of ideas and inspiration. You become more creative, innovative, and fresh ideas flow naturally and effortlessly.

But when you're doing what you dislike, you're easily discouraged, irritated and bored. People who are trapped in jobs or careers they weren't created to do get easily tired and disinterested in their jobs. It becomes mundane and unstimulating for them. They start hopping from one job to another because they are bored.

So, what do you love? What do you enjoy? What stirs up your creativity and enthusiasm? Take some time now with your journal and write down everything you can think of that fits those questions. Now, when you draw up your list, you'll most likely produce a long one.

For instance, you love gardening, plumbing, music, architecture, children, mathematics, etc. This will leave you wondering which one is truly connected to your purpose. Not to worry, we're going to sift them to determine the right one. As humans, we love so many things, but your purpose is hidden in those things you love with a strong passion.

What's Your Passion?

Humans are creatures of emotion. We express emotions in varying degrees. Sometimes, the emotions are casual, but other times, they are deep and intense. When we exhibit deep and intense emotions, sometimes uncontrollably, we're being passionate. In life, there are things that evoke strong emotions in us. These emotions may be positive or negative. Your life's purpose is hidden in the things you love or hate with a passion.

When I ask the question, "What do you love?" I want you to know that I'm referring to the things you love with so much passion that you're moved to act. The same applies to the things you hate. There are things you hate so much they move you to act. They may include injustice, corruption, hunger, bad leadership, and abuse – usually societal problems. These problems touch you so deeply that you're provoked to change the status quo. Although you may not have the resources to effect a change, you desperately wish you could do something about it. These passions are pointers towards your life purpose.

Oh, but everyone loves or hates similar things, you may think. Who doesn't love sports? And who doesn't hate injustice or child abuse and so forth? Yes, one may love or hate those things, but the difference is that their love or hatred doesn't spur them to act. They may admire or condemn something, but that's where they stop. They don't take any further step to do something about it.

Now, regarding your list, you're going to cross out those things you don't love with a strong passion. To help you understand your passions better, let's discuss some telltale signs that you're passionate about something.

You are Obsessed with it

Your passions are hidden in the things you love so much that it consumes and overwhelms you. You hardly notice the passage of time when you're at it. Now, I'm not talking about frivolous things like chatting on social media, watching movies, or making long phone calls. No, those are time killers. Instead, I'm referring to productive activities that consume you. Your purpose may be hidden in those activities.

Let's take a look at Michael. Long before he enrolled in the university, it was obvious to his family what he was created to do. As a young boy, Michael was a menace to every electronic appliance in their home. He was fascinated by every gadget and would rip them apart to find out how they worked.

First, he started with the wall clocks. He spent hours gazing at the big grandfather clock in their sitting room, wondering how it worked. Unfortunately, he didn't ask his parents any of the questions that baffled him. Instead, he attempted to get the answers by himself. He ended up dismantling all the clocks, but then couldn't re-assemble them.

Afterwards, he moved on to the electric irons, radios, blenders, and damaged every single one of them. Despite punishments from his parents, his curiosity never waned, and he moved from one item to another, leaving damaged gadgets in his wake. His siblings were mad at him because he destroyed every entertainment appliance, which included the TV, VCR / VCD players, computer games and so on.

No electronic device survived the curious mind and untrained fingers of their brother. They began locking up some of these appliances, but he managed to sneak into the rooms when no one was watching, to conduct his experiments.

When Michael couldn't control his curiosity anymore, he visited an electrical store near their residence, to watch the technicians repairing appliances. Young Michael went into a certain man's shop, sat down, and began to observe his work, without explaining who he was or the reason for his visit. Luckily, the store owner wasn't a bad person and saw no harm in the gentle-looking boy. Michael sat quietly from morning to evening, without saying a word to the technician or getting in his way.

He repeated the visit for a week, and, after that, his curiosity was satisfied. Michael returned to every item he had damaged in the previous years and began to fix them. He convinced his mum to buy certain tools for him and, using them, he fixed everything. He became so good that neighbors called on him to fix their faulty electronic appliances, too. Michael was only twelve years old!

Seeing the transformation, Michael's dad encouraged him to study hard so he could get into university to perfect his talents. He did and, today, Michael is an Electrical, Electronic and Computer Engineer.

Michael's obsession with electronic devices was a pointer that his purpose had to do with engineering or some kind of technical vocation. He spent hours upon hours working on those contraptions. Even when they were locked up, he couldn't control himself. While his mates were playing games, Michael was sitting in someone's shop, trying to learn how to fix electronic gadgets.

You see, Michael wasn't only obsessed with electronic gadgets, he also lost track of time, forgot meals, and disregarded the pain of punishment from his parents. He just couldn't control himself; his passion drove him.

Can you imagine Michael as a medical doctor or an accountant? If he became a medical doctor by chance, he would be more interested in how the MRI machine worked, rather than his patient's response to treatment! So those topics that you're engrossed, obsessed or pre-occupied with, beyond the ordinary, are your passions and the clues to your life purpose. Oh, by the way, Michael is my younger brother!

You Talk about it a Lot

Another clue to discovering your passions are those topics that captivate you so much, you think or talk about them all the time. Others around you may not care about those topics, but you do. In fact, you may bore and irritate them, because they don't share your passion in those topics. But you can't stop yourself from talking, even if no one wants to listen!

When you see a book or magazine on the topic, you quickly read it. And when you hear it on TV or radio, you sit up and listen. You search the internet for more information on this subject. You watch YouTube videos and read blogs or articles, to understand the topic better. These reactions are not ordinary; they are pointers that your purpose may be hidden in that topic.

I visited a 94-year-old lady some time ago with a colleague. She lived alone, was strong and independent. On entering her living room, I saw a bookshelf. Since I'm always drawn to books, I later stepped aside to take a closer look. Apart from a few bibles and two or three volumes of Christian literature, all the books were culinary books. I was fascinated! There were over two hundred of them. Do I need to tell you her purpose or what she did with those 94 years?

Similarly, my library holds a clue to my purpose. Besides my pharmacy textbooks, all the books in my library fall under two subjects. Just two. When I visit the public library, I gravitate towards a certain section and when I go to the bookstore, the same thing happens. Why? It's my purpose pulling me towards those topics.

What are these topics? Inquiring minds want to know. They include personal development and religion. I read, listen to, teach and write about them all the time. In fact, more than pharmacy. Since I have a passion to help young people develop into greater versions of themselves, I am drawn to these topics.

I watched a short video of a little boy who was so captivated by a subject, it was obvious that his purpose was tied to it. Although he was only about five years old, this boy's love for airplanes drove him to accumulate knowledge only experts are aware of. He knew the workings of an airplane, names, and functions of all the parts in the cockpit. But more importantly, he had studied the technology behind each part and compared it to older ones.

As I explained earlier, your purpose is hidden in what you often talk about. So, this boy shared his knowledge of the workings of an airplane with a flight attendant, who was so impressed, she brought him into the cockpit to share his enthusiasm with the pilots. What an opportunity! In the video, the boy pointed out several parts and explained their functions, while fielding questions from the amazed pilots. Of course, you can easily guess what his career desire is – to become a pilot.

Your life purpose is hidden in you. It's within you. But it seeks expression through the things you do. When you hear a particular topic mentioned, it seems to kick within you, like a baby kicks in its mother's womb. That's why you gravitate towards certain topics that are connected to your purpose. You may wonder why your siblings are not interested in the same topics. They are not, because they don't carry the same purpose within them.

Your life purpose can be likened to a magnet within you. A magnet attracts certain materials but repels or remains neutral to others. Similarly, your purpose is like a magnet within you that pulls you towards certain topics, subjects and careers that relate to it, but remains neutral to others. So, when you discover a pull or an inclination towards certain subjects, don't ignore it. It could be your purpose in action.

Some of us ignore these inclinations and assume they are insignificant or ordinary. That's a mistake because these inclinations are pointers to your purpose. You're passionate about those topics you talk, think, watch, and read about all the time and they are pointers to your life purpose.

Your Curiosity is Aroused

Your passion is exposed through your curiosity. From the stories I've shared, you'll notice that curiosity runs across them. There was always an insatiable quest for more knowledge regarding the topic. Excessive curiosity about a subject is a clue to your passion and to your purpose. It was the clue that led me to accidentally discover my purpose.

As long as I could remember, I was curious about drugs. I wondered what they were made of and how they worked. When I had a headache, my mum would give me a tablet to take. I was surprised that, although the tablet went into my stomach, somehow it managed to stop the ache in my head. How did it know that the pain was in my head and how did it get there? These questions ran through my six-year-old brain, and I was mystified.

As I grew older, whenever I went to the hospital, the doctors educated me about my treatments.

This heightened my curiosity and I wanted to know the drug for every medical condition. My family and I misinterpreted my passion and we all accepted that I would become a medical doctor.

It was settled and I knew my path for life, but years later, I realized something was amiss because I couldn't stand the sight of blood. In fact, I must confess that, even today, when I watch TV shows or movies where there's an accident or surgery, exposing flesh and bones mingled with blood, I surreptitiously look away! Evidently, I was not designed to be a doctor.

As I got ready to apply to university, I knew it couldn't be for medicine and surgery. I was confused. I began to seek answers from outsiders. Computer science was hot at that time, so I enrolled for that. I was headed down the wrong path.

A year later, I'd had a lot of time for reflection, and I realized that my passion and curiosity had to do with drugs and not the human body. And the field of learning that catered to it was pharmacy. Ignoring misconceptions then, that pharmacy was for those who failed to get into medical school, I went for my passion. And I'm glad to be a drug specialist!

What topic captivates your curiosity to the extent that you can't imagine living your life without your curiosity being satisfied? For me, I realized I would never be happy or fulfilled, if I didn't know the drug therapy for every medical condition. I couldn't imagine a life without that knowledge! What's yours? Are you curious about wealth and how to make it? About plants and how they grow? You'll know that curiosity is a clue to your purpose when it's strong enough to move you to act.

You Take Action

Hopefully, you're crossing out more items from your list because you can separate what you love from what you're passionate about. Another way to differentiate your passion from the things you merely love is to identify those things that you love so much they spur you to act. You take certain steps because you don't just love it, you're passionate about it.

Many people are sports lovers. For example, most Nigerians are intoxicated with soccer, especially the European leagues. They are fans of Arsenal, Manchester United, Barcelona, you name them! They discuss football, watch it, and forgo important meetings when the timing clashes. They place bets, hold thanksgiving services in churches when their favorite teams win and celebrate wildly. I can confidently say that soccer is the opium of many Nigerians.

Yet, despite their enthusiasm for the sport, it usually ends there – in their sitting rooms, clubs or viewing centers. They take no further action to pursue a career in football - except for a handful. Football for the majority is all about entertainment. It does not stir them to act. This isn't unique to Nigerians it cuts across the entire world.

However, some individuals love soccer so much, they cannot imagine a life without it. These are the likes of Lionel Messi, Cristiano Ronaldo, and other young men and women, who entertain us on the field. The difference is that football isn't just entertainment to them, they acted because it's their purpose for life. Purpose isn't just what you love, but what moves you to act.

So, what are the passions that have moved you to act in the past? Have you been talking, reading, and spending hours learning more about them? Which of your passions would you love to spend the rest of your life doing? Is it singing, painting, taking care of older people, flying airplanes, or playing football? These questions will help you discover your purpose through your passions.

However, just in case you're not passionate about any topic to the degree I have explained, don't lose hope. It could be that your purpose is not hidden in your positive passions. It may be hidden in those things you hate with a passion. Join me in the next chapter as we explore this interesting clue to discovering your life's purpose.

The Golden Nuggets

- ➤ Life purpose is hidden in things you love with a passion.
- ➤ Your passions are those things that stir up deep emotions, positive or negative.
- ➤ Doing the thing you love infuses you with energy, innovation, and fresh ideas.
- ➤ Doing what you dislike saps your strength and leaves you bored.
- ➤ Your passions are in those things you're obsessed with.
- ➤ Your passions are those things that make you forget time, meals, or friends.
- ➤ Your passions are in those things you think, talk, watch, or read about all the time.
- ➤ Your passions are in those things that move you to act.

Study Exercises

➢ How can you separate what you love from what you're passionate about?

➢ What do you love? List them.

➢ Which ones are you obsessed with?

➢ Which ones make you forget time, meals, people, or other activities?

➢ Which topics do you talk about all the time?

➢ Which topics do you have a lot of related books, videos, magazines about?

➢ What topics do you watch on TV, YouTube, or social media?

➢ Which topics have you ever attended a conference or lecture on?

➢ Which item on your list do you have heroes from?

➢ Those items that made the checklist are your passions. Arrange them from the strongest to the weakest.

Chapter 6

What do you Hate?

"There is a time to love and a time to hate."
—King Solomon

L ife isn't all about love, according to the wise sage, King Solomon. There are certain things that deserve hatred. Not fellow humans, or animals, but ills such as injustice, corruption, hunger, etc. What do you hate? And just as we established in the previous chapter, I'm referring to things you hate with such a deep passion, they spur you to act. They could be a pointer to your purpose.

Life is synonymous with problems. We cannot avoid it. The only problem-free zone is the grave.

But so long as we're alive, we're constantly confronted with one problem or another. We need people who are passionately angry about these problems, to get them solved.

Millions have heard that many children starve to death, and they hate it. Millions have also heard of the negative impacts of domestic violence, and they resent it. However, that's all they've done – to hate it. But they don't hate it enough to act. Therefore, they are not candidates to bring about change.

According to American author and speaker, Dr. Mike Murdock, whatever you can tolerate, you cannot change. Although most people hate the problems in our society, they can tolerate them. But some people cannot. These problems bother them so much, they search for avenues to eradicate them. That's a clue to life purpose. Purpose is hidden in those things you hate so much they move you to act.

She Confronted a Problem

Malala Yousafzai is a Pakistani girl, who is the youngest recipient of the Nobel Peace Prize for her work in addressing the problem of education in her country. At the early age of eleven, Malala gave her first speech opposing the Taliban's attempt to deny girls formal education in Pakistan.

The Taliban had closed many girls' schools and blown up about a hundred others. Malala became an activist, working closely with the British Broadcasting Corporation (BBC to raise awareness of the problem going on in her country.

Her activism led to many TV appearances, both local and international, and meetings with influential world leaders. On her way back from school one day, Malala was shot in the head by the Taliban. The fifteen-year-old survived the gruesome attack after undergoing many surgeries. This led to more protests and increased international awareness that ultimately caused the Pakistani government to ratify a bill that allowed young girls access to formal education.

Malala saw a problem, but unlike other Pakistanis who saw the same problem, she was deeply stirred to do something. At her young age, she could only raise awareness and attract the attention of political leaders, who could solve the problem. This is purpose in action. Just like Malala, what are the problems you hate so much, you want to help cause a change? It may not be as huge as what she confronted, but it could be the problem you were created to solve.

What Angers You?

Sometimes, certain problems evoke a different type of emotion from you. Instead of hate, you feel anger. Some of you are angry with your corrupt leaders and wish you could take their place and provide better governance. Some of you are angry with the hospital system in your country and desire to make a change. Some are angry about the rising death rate from drug and substance abuse.

A distinctive point is that people around you don't share this anger to the same degree. Sure, they may not like what is going on, but they are not prompted to change the situation. Some may even complain that you're over-reacting. No, you're not. It's your purpose that's tugging at you.

Like a fetus in the womb, it's kicking and won't let you rest till you begin to take definite action towards it. It's calling you to rise and take personal responsibility to confront the problems that anger you and produce a change.

We learnt in the previous chapter that your purpose is about serving humanity and making life better for others. When you experience these emotions, you must rise to the occasion and take responsibility for a change. You will never be fulfilled in life till you discover the problems you're here to solve. Fulfillment demands you live for a cause higher than you. It demands you live a life that will lift others to a higher ground.

Nelson Mandela, Mahatma Gandhi, and Martin Luther King Jnr are examples of men who took personal responsibility to challenge the problems of leadership in their countries. There are individuals who have taken responsibility to confront problems such as cancer, texting-while-driving, domestic violence and so on. Is there any problem you're highly driven to confront?

The Intersection of Your Love and Hate

Your purpose could be found at the intersection of your love and your hate. You may be confused by the conflicting emotions you experience but I'm here to provide some clarity. For instance, you love your country, but at the same time, you feel that you hate the same country. How can you love and hate your country at the same time? It's your purpose that is gnawing at you.

You do love your country, and your hatred isn't really directed at your country per se, but at the corruption, injustices, poor administration, or other ills going on in your country. It could be directed at the mismanagement of resources, poor leadership, and governance.

Your purpose is hidden at this intersection. It is a call to step forward in any capacity, to resolve some of these issues because of your love for your country.

Let's look at another example. You love marriage. You love the idea of falling in love, getting married and raising a family. But on the other hand, you're getting cold feet about marriage. The stories you hear make you criticize marriage and some of the things associated with marriage. Listening to you, one may wonder why you hate marriage. But you really don't.

What you hate are the problems associated with the marriage institution. Problems such as domestic violence, emotional and physical abuse, inequality and infringement of human rights directed at some spouses trigger your hatred. Your response is heightened because it is connected to your purpose.

Let's say you love children, but you hate the abuse surrounding children. Child trafficking, child labor and child abuse tear at your heart. This has a profound effect on you because, deep within, maybe unknown to you, is an unquenchable love for children. Your purpose is a call to stand up for these little ones in any way you can.

You cannot stand up to fight for a nation you don't love. You can't rise up to fix an institution you don't love. It is your love that is at the root of your actions. Your hate is stirred up because of your love. While your hate motivates you to take a step, your love will sustain you as you strive to accomplish your purpose. Just as Nelson Mandela's love for his country sustained him as he spent 27 years in prison.

What do you hate? And what do you love? What's their intersection? That intersection is a pointer towards your purpose.

Your Past Experiences

In addition to what you hate and what angers you, your life's purpose could be hidden in the experiences of your life. Sometimes, your personal experiences ignite a passion of hate or anger against certain issues. Oftentimes, we're nonchalant about the sufferings of others, until it affects us. That's when we realize that millions have been suffering and it needs to stop. Thus, our past experiences and our background could hold keys to revealing our purpose in life.

What significant life experiences have stirred your passion of hate or anger to effect a change? For some of you, it may not have happened to you but to a family member or a close friend. But such experiences have knocked you out of your comfort zone and kindled a huge passion about it.

Texting-while-driving is a dangerous activity, popular among teens. It has claimed a lot of young lives. Although the government is vocal against it, some parents have also raised their voices through various avenues to confront the issue. This happened after experiencing the anguish of losing their children to texting-while-driving related car accidents.

Some people have lost loved ones to certain illnesses, which drove them to take up careers in the medical field to help others. Some set up nonprofit organizations to raise awareness and resources to tackle those diseases. Some, having faced the problem of injustice, chose a career in law to help victims of injustice. Some women experienced teen pregnancy and, today, they help teen moms cope with their challenges.

Therefore, don't disregard your past experiences because your purpose could be hidden in them. You may need to review your painful struggles to discover your purpose. Then commit yourself to fighting that cause because that's the reason you were born!

Our world needs people who will passionately confront problems and bring about solutions.

The world is awaiting people who hate certain problems, people who are angered by certain problems or people with traumatic experiences, to rise up and bring succor to those who are still suffering.

By the way, what's your temperament? Are you introverted or extroverted? Your temperament is an interesting clue to discover your life purpose. Come with me as I show you how.

The Golden Nuggets

➢ Your purpose may be hidden in the things you hate with a passion – mainly life problems.

➢ Your passionate hatred for these problems moves you to act.

➢ Purpose is found at the intersection of your love and your hate. While your hate drives you to act, your love sustains you.

➢ The world needs people who are passionately driven by hate or anger to confront certain problems.

➢ Some traumatic life experiences hold the clue to your purpose.

➢ Sometimes people recognize a problem because they have experienced it.

➢ You must rise up to bring a solution to the problems you were created to resolve.

Study Exercises

➢ What do you hate with such a passion, it pushes you to act?

➢ What angers you to the extent you're moved to act?

➢ Can you identify something you both love and hate and find the intersection of both?

➢ If you had the resources to effect a change, what problem would you tackle?

➢ Did you have a bitter life experience that stirs up passion against something? What is that thing?

➢ Is there a problem that you're completely obsessed to resolve?

➢ Is there a problem you're always complaining, thinking, or reading about and would want to change?

Chapter 7

What are Your Strengths?

"Talent can't be taught but it can be awakened."
—Wallace Stegner, American novelist, and
winner of the Pulitzer Prize.

Everyone born into this world is endowed with certain abilities, gifts, or talents. These inherent abilities are part of a design to enable us to accomplish our purpose with ease.

Back to our animal analogy, the bird is designed with wings that make flying effortless. The fish is designed with fins that make swimming easy. Similarly, every human is endowed with gifts and talents that make certain tasks easy and effortless. Therefore, these abilities can be used as clues to determine one's purpose, because often they reveal the task one is created to perform – their life purpose.

"Oh, but I'm not talented!" you might say.

Oh yes, you are. In this chapter, we're going to look at the various abilities you possess, which may not initially appear as talents. And by the time we're done, you'll be amazed at the strengths you possess. So, get your journal and pencil ready because you'll have a lot to write.

What are Your Natural Abilities?

As mentioned earlier, your natural abilities, gifts or talents are usually tied to your purpose. They are designed to enable you fulfill your purpose with ease. What abilities come easily to you, unlike your siblings and friends? What are you a natural at?

Let's start by taking a trip down memory lane to your childhood and list the things you did so well, you received a lot of compliments. Oftentimes, in our childhood, we're uninhibited and tend to express ourselves freely. We're neither self-conscious nor aware of negative criticisms, so we express our gifts and abilities spontaneously. Go ahead and write them down.

Don't ignore abilities such as culinary skills, organizational abilities, leadership potential, ability to motivate or inspire others. And don't take abilities such as dancing, reading, negotiation, eloquence, or storytelling for granted. Anything you can do relatively well and seemingly effortlessly compared to others should be noted.

It's important to mention that, while some abilities are pretty obvious, others aren't. So, it takes a keen eye to spot them. Jumping around the house, hopping across furniture and objects isn't a talent, is it? But when she displayed these skills before a trained eye, the greatest gymnast of all time was discovered.

This chance meeting happened during a daycare field trip to a gymnasium when Simone was six years old. She saw some girls practicing their gymnastic routines on beams and trampolines. They were flipping and tumbling, and she began to imitate them.

A coach came over and questioned if she had ever done that before. Then she sent a letter to Simone's parents, informing them that she had observed a natural talent in their daughter and encouraging them to enroll her for proper training.

That was the beginning of a journey that would turn young Simone Biles into the most decorated American gymnast and the world's third most decorated gymnast, with 32 Olympic and World Championship medals!

Your talent may not be easily recognizable, simply because it's still in a crude form. Nonetheless, it's still a talent. What if Simone's parents had doubted the coach because Simone wasn't an obvious gymnast? They understood that talent comes in crude form, like a dirty piece of rock, but with work, it can be polished into a beautiful diamond.

Just in case you're still wondering what your talents could be, they are things you can do relatively well without prior preparation or training. Just like Simone, who hadn't been trained to flip and tumble, but she pulled it off so well that a coach noticed.

You may be naturally good at many things, and that's great. Don't disregard any of them because they play significant roles in your earthly assignment. Your strengths may be your purpose or an aide to your purpose.

Your purpose may demand several skillsets; that's why you may be born with numerous abilities. Therefore, don't disregard any talent you have. List them and we'll look for their connection to your purpose.

What is Your Temperament?

Besides your talents, your temperament endows you with certain abilities and strengths. These abilities come naturally to you, simply because of your temperament. For instance, while one person may struggle with relating to people, another finds it amazingly easy to mingle with people, including strangers. Without prior training and environmental considerations, the difference between these people can be traced to their temperament.

Your temperament tells a lot about who you are and explains why you act in a certain way. It's responsible for certain natural tendencies and aptitudes. While some are positive or strengths, others are weaknesses. Your temperament determines why you think like you think, feel like you feel and act like you act.

But first, what is temperament? Temperament is defined as the peculiar or distinguishing mental or physical character of an individual. It's the genetically inherited behavioral tendencies that are a part of our DNA and are independent of learning, values, or attitudes.

Simply put, your temperament is why you act the way you do. It's your inherent design, your internal wiring. Although you can modify some aspects, you cannot change it, because it's who you are. It's usually best to improve on the weaknesses of your temperament, though.

Since your temperament reveals your innate abilities, we shall study and discover your temperament and, by extension, use it as a clue to discover your purpose. Your temperament is a bolster to your assignment. It's a natural endowment to help you achieve your purpose with ease. Therefore, understanding your temperament is a key to revealing the assignment you're here to complete.

There are four types of temperaments. They are Sanguine, Choleric, Melancholy and Phlegmatic. The first two are extroverts, while the latter are introverts. Tim LaHaye, in his book 'Why You

Act the Way You Do' and Dr D.W. Ekstrand in his article, "The Four Human Temperaments," describe these four temperaments in great details.

Sanguine

The Sanguine is an extrovert who enjoys and thrives around people. They are the life of a party, talkers who enter a room with their mouth first and can strike up conversations easily with anyone. They love to be the center of attention, cheerful, pleasant, enthusiastic, and full of energy. They are creative, humorous, sincere at heart, colorful and enjoy making people happy. They are social butterflies.

They love people and thrive on compliments. They are optimistic, lively, and fun to be with. They make the world a happy place. Due to their sociable and charismatic nature, Sanguine thrive in careers where they interact with people. They make good salespersons.

They love adventure and spontaneity and are easily bored with routine and monotony. They also love activities requiring preparation and energy. Therefore, monotonous jobs aren't suited for a Sanguine. They also prefer group activities, rather than solo projects. On the flip side, the Sanguine is notorious for not completing tasks, habitually late, disorganized, and tends to neglect their obligations.

Choleric

The Choleric is the natural leader, hard-driving individual, known for accomplishing goals. They are aggressive, tenacious, decisive, and very independent. Choleric are also strong-willed, forceful, and passionate about their pursuits and try to instill same in their followers. They love to be in control and thrive in careers where they have authority and can supervise others. They can be bossy and domineering, driving their subordinates to achieve goals and meet deadlines.

Negatively, they are impatient, hot-tempered, easily angered, and unsympathetic. They enjoy arguments and can dominate others, especially the Phlegmatic. They are workaholics, who are not swayed by adversities; in fact, they thrive on them. They make great military and political figures.

Choleric are emotionally insensitive. They are the least emotionally developed of all the temperaments. They don't sympathize easily and are more often irritated by tears and displays of weakness or vulnerability. So, they don't thrive in careers that require human compassion. (You don't want to encounter a Choleric nurse on your sick day! And due to their strong leadership tendencies, they thrive in the military, politics, as CEOs, entrepreneurs and other positions of leadership.

Melancholy

The Melancholy is an introverted personality type, who is thoughtful, detailed, highly analytical and well-organized. They are perfectionists, purposeful, serious, conscientious, neat, and disciplined. They are extraordinarily talented in music, literature, and arts. They are philosophical, creative, and endowed with high IQ. They make the best scientists, inventors and artists, vocations where perfection is required.

Because they are emotionally sensitive and caring, they make good doctors, nurses, social workers and teachers. Their great attention to detail makes them good accountants, architects, surgeons or chemists. And due to their shy or timid nature, they don't thrive as public speakers, salespersons or in positions that keep them in the spotlight, unlike the Sanguine.

Phlegmatic

The Phlegmatic is an introverted personality, who is known for being very calm, easy-going, and sluggish. They are cool, nice, less adventurous in life, somewhat lazy and content to just flow with everything and everyone. They are tolerant, never in a hurry, peaceful and witty. Their agreeable nature wins them a lot of friends and their witty, easygoing, unassuming nature makes them good company.

They avoid conflict and usually hide their emotions. Due to their warm, trusting, rational, observant, sympathetic and consistent nature, they make excellent administrators and teachers. Due to their sluggish nature, and preference to be uninvolved, they rarely make great leaders or innovators.

Your Temperament is a Clue

I love how Tim LaHaye describes the four temperaments teaching a group of six-year-olds. The Phlegmatic would make the best teacher because they are patient and calm with the children. The Sanguine will keep the children entertained by telling them one story after another. The Melancholy will criticize them for failing to meet their perfectionist standards, while the Choleric will cause the children to leap out of the window!

This is why your purpose could be hidden in your temperament!

Your temperament is a strong clue to discovering your purpose. If you're a Sanguine, your purpose is tied to activities that involve people. You were designed to be around people, not holed up in some office, poring over numbers and graphs. But if you hate being around people, that's okay, because it's likely you're an introvert, designed to spend hours with inanimate objects, searching for solutions or creating a masterpiece.

I worked with a Sanguine at one time, in pharmaceutical marketing. I was amazed by his ability to connect with strangers. This colleague entered offices with his mouth first and got everyone laughing. By the time he announced his intentions, it was an easy pass. A Melancholy, on the other hand, will steal into the room, trying extremely hard not to be seen by anyone.

While marketing may be an easy pass for the Sanguine, it will demand a lot of energy for the Melancholy. As a result, while the Sanguine is rejuvenated after a long day of work, the Melancholy is strained. He is exerting too much energy to achieve comparable results.

The Choleric is a natural leader, designed to be less sensitive to human feelings, so as to make quick decisions, drive end points and accomplish goals. While others work hard to horn their leadership skills, it comes naturally to the Choleric. Whereas the others develop strategies to motivate and encourage themselves to achieve goals, it's a walk in the park for the Choleric.

The Phlegmatic is calm and good with administration. His organizational skills are in-born. He is Mr. Efficient. Thus, he can administrate a firm easily. The same applies to the Melancholy, who is very meticulous and disciplined. However, this type of task will impose a strain on the Sanguine, who is naturally disorganized and forgetful. He will jumble up schedules, miss appointments and create a chaotic mess, but his good nature will be his saving grace.

So, what's your temperament? Are you a people person (Sanguine), a leader (Choleric), a thinker (Melancholy), or a jolly good fellow (Phlegmatic)? What comes easily to you, as a result of your temperament? What can you do, based on your temperament? What is a stretch or strain on your abilities and what's not? Your temperament will enable you achieve your purpose without undue strain.

Dear intelligent reader, did you know that your unique intelligence is a clue to unravelling your life purpose? Not to worry, I'm going to show you how. Let's jump on to it!

Golden Nuggets

> ➤ Natural abilities, such as gifts or talents, are clues to your purpose.

> ➤ Your talents are found in things you do well without prior training or preparation.

> ➤ Your temperament holds your natural strengths and weaknesses.

> ➤ There are four major types of temperament: Sanguine, Choleric, Melancholy and Phlegmatic.

> ➤ Your temperament explains your capacity for certain abilities and deficiencies, too.

Study Exercises

➤ What are your talents and strengths? Make a list.

➤ What can you do that those around you find difficult?

➤ If you were woken up and asked to do it, what would you do and still get compliments?

➤ Although you've not been trained, what can you do relatively well?

➤ What is your temperament?

➤ Based on your temperament, what comes naturally to you? And what is a huge strain on you?

➤ Look at your list. Are there passions that run parallel to or opposite to your temperament?

Chapter 8

What's Your Intelligence?

"It's not how smart you are that matters, what really counts is how you are smart."
—Howard Gardner.

How are you intelligent? Yes, how? Are you intelligent with human relationships or with mathematics? Are you intelligent in the sports arena or in the classroom? Are you disposed to working mentally or physically? Are you a hands-on person, bookworm, or computer geek?

Before I confuse you further with these questions, let me offer some explanations.

For a long time, the concept of intelligence was restricted to one area - Logical-Mathematical. Students were labelled intelligent or unintelligent, based on their performance in the classroom alone. The standard metric was their performance in the intelligence-quotient (IQ) test. Students with high IQ scores were deemed smart and intelligent, whereas those with low scores were not.

Academic brilliance doesn't translate to excellence in sports, music, or theatre. Do we imply that a person who isn't good in the classroom but is highly proficient in other fields isn't intelligent? Does it mean the athlete who performs nerve-wracking twists and turns midair isn't intelligent, because they cannot solve a quadratic equation?

Some kids who aren't physically energetic, or hands-on at projects that involve manual skills are often labelled lazy and incompetent. Usually, they prefer studying to working manually, they'd rather be researching on their computers than playing sports. They excel in the classroom but can hardly join two pieces of wood together with a nail and a hammer.

Are they truly lazy and incompetent?

These scenarios led Howard Gardner, a developmental psychologist to question the intelligence tests used in the school system, which measured only a student's logical and mathematical abilities, popularly known as IQ tests. He proposed the theory of multiple intelligences, since it takes a different type of intelligence to excel in math, sports, interpersonal relationships and so on.

He redefined our Interpretation of intelligence to accommodate various areas of aptitude. Thus, it's no longer how smart you are, but how you are smart. Are you smart with words or with people? Are you smart athletically or scientifically? Are you designed to work physically or mentally?

Your unique intelligence is a strength to help you achieve your purpose. Therefore, your intelligence could be a pointer towards your life purpose.

Gardner's Theory of Multiple Intelligences

In his book, 'Frames of Mind: The Theory of Multiple Intelligences,' developmental psychologist Howard Gardner proposed nine types of intelligences, as opposed to one. They are:

1. **Linguistic Intelligence (Word smart)** : As the name implies, it means one is good with words, languages, and communication. People with this type of intelligence make good journalists, lawyers, writers, motivational speakers, etc.

2. **Musical Intelligence (Music smart)** : This deals with skills in performance and composition of music and sounds. It embodies everything musical. Careers in this field of intelligence include singers, composers, DJs, etc.

3. **Bodily-Kinesthetic Intelligence (Body smart)** : This refers to the ability to coordinate the body in physical activities. Body smart individuals 'learn with their hands' – physical learning. They include athletes, craftspeople, dancers, etc.

4. **Existential Intelligence (Life smart)** : This type of intelligence deals with abstract subjects, theological or philosophical ideas. They are intuitive, and concerned with life, human existence, or religion. Life smart people include philosophers, theologians, life coaches, etc.

5. **Naturalistic Intelligence (Nature smart)** : This pertains to nature. These are nature lovers, who are interested in plants, animals, insects, mountains, etc. Nature smart people specialize in careers such as geology, botany, agriculture, geography, etc.

6. **Interpersonal (Emotional) Intelligence (People smart)** : This type of intelligence deals with human relationships. It's

understanding how people feel and being able to empathize with them. People smart individuals are good at analyzing human relationships and they make good counsellors, salespeople, public relations workers, etc.

7. **Logical-Mathematical Intelligence (Number/Reasoning smart)** : This is the common intelligence, usually measured with IQ tests. It deals with reasoning and numbers, as the name depicts. Some people have a remarkably high IQ, while others don't. They make good scientists, researchers, doctors, teachers, etc.

8. **Intrapersonal Intelligence (Self-smart)** : This type of intelligence deals with self-awareness. The ability to understand oneself – your fears, drives, abilities, weaknesses, goals, and purpose. In fact, by reading this book, you're improving your intrapersonal intelligence. Self-smart people make good philosophers,

entrepreneurs, counselors, and spiritual leaders.

9. **Visual-Spatial Intelligence (Picture smart):** This pertains to the ability to visualize with the mind's eye, imagine or create abstract ideas in three dimensions. These people make renowned artists, architects, builders, etc.

From Gardner's theory of multiple intelligence, you can figure out what type of smart you are. Are you self-smart or body smart? Are you good at interpersonal relationships or can you visualize and create abstracts in three dimensions? So, go ahead and write down your intelligences.

With this newfound knowledge, you may now cease comparing yourself with others. There's no need to feel intimidated because someone can spell all the words in the dictionary. That's their intelligence. You've got yours and they can't compete with you in that area. Your intelligence can help you to serve your life purpose. Do you see a clue based on your intelligence(s)?

The Convergence

In this and the previous chapter, you deeply analyzed yourself. You discovered your talents, both obvious and non-obvious. You've also gone down memory lane to unravel the abilities you'd buried.

Furthermore, you've learnt about the various temperaments and may have identified yours. And finally, you've decided on the type of intelligence(s) you possess. All these inherent abilities, aptitudes and dispositions are tailored to enable you fulfill your purpose with ease.

With these written down, can you see where they converge? What do they point to? Are they pointing to any passion you listed in the previous chapter? What passion is it?

Let's analyze Toby. He is a Sanguine, who loves to be around people. Since he was a little boy, he's had a passion for cars – electric cars, diesel cars, fast cars. In addition, Toby is people smart;

he knows how to make people feel good about themselves. Toby needs to explore opportunities related to cars and people.

Precious is a Melancholy, who is emotionally sensitive. She has linguistic intelligence – word smart. While growing up, Precious witnessed some girls in her community being kidnapped and sold into sex trafficking. It left an indelible scar on her sensitive soul. As a result, she hates trafficking with a passion.

For Precious, resolving the problem of sex trafficking will be aided by her linguistic abilities. Since she is word smart, she could use her voice or writings to create awareness. A legal career or a non-profit organization could be avenues for her to cater to the needs of the victims of trafficking.

In a comparable way, put your passions, talents, hobbies, temperament, and intelligences together and see what you arrive at. Did it reveal your life purpose? If you're not sure, that's fine.

You still have several chapters to learn more clues to discover your purpose.

Tired? I hope not! Let's hop on to the next chapter and talk about your uniqueness as a clue to discovering your life purpose.

Golden Nuggets

- ➢ IQ is not a true measure of intelligence.
- ➢ There are nine distinct types of intelligence, according to Gardner.
- ➢ Your intelligence reveals your innate strength and abilities.
- ➢ Your intelligence is a pointer towards your purpose.
- ➢ The convergence of your talents, temperament, intelligence, and passions points to your life purpose.

Study Exercises

- ➤ What is/are your intelligence(s)?
- ➤ What passions align with your intelligence(s)?
- ➤ Based on the information you've discovered about yourself, what should you be doing? And what should you not be doing?
- ➤ Should you be in your current job or studies, based on your discoveries about yourself?
- ➤ What is the convergence of your talents, temperament, intelligence, and passions? What are they pointing to?
- ➤ Try analyzing some people you know very well. See if you can identify the convergence their talents, hobbies, temperaments, intelligences, and passions, to arrive at their purpose. This is not for their information, it's just an exercise to help you master the subject.

Chapter 9

What's Your Uniqueness?

"What sets you apart can sometimes feel like a burden and it's not. And a lot of the time, it's what makes you great." —Emma Stone

"Professor, bookworm, over-sabi," they snickered as Ike walked down the aisle to his seat, after receiving yet another prize for his academic excellence. Ike was a gentle boy, who was bullied because of his extraordinary intellectual abilities. He was called names, laughed at, and had few friends. He couldn't help being extremely intelligent since he was born that way. But some of his classmates made him so miserable that Ike took drastic measures to overcome his misery.

He stopped doing his homework and, when asked questions, he gave the wrong answers. He tried extremely hard to become average and, if possible, flunk just to gain acceptance. Ike's teacher couldn't understand his sudden mediocre performance.

Her conversations with him yielded nothing, so she reported the problem to his parents. Her best student had turned into a dullard! Despite his efforts to gain acceptance, Ike's classmates were not deceived. They knew he was different from everyone else.

Unfortunately, Ike's attempts to reject his uniqueness brought about a major setback in his life. His delinquency resulted in failure to get placement into the secondary school of his dreams. Ike was mortified! He broke down and revealed his ordeals to his parents. To salvage his future, Ike's parents withdrew and enrolled him in a different school, where he repeated the class and passed with flying colors.

We are created differently from one another. We are unique in our fingerprints and DNA sequence. However, some individuals are so markedly different in certain areas that it sets them apart from others. They stand out from the pack. Their distinctiveness sets them apart so much that it puts them in the spotlight. As a result, they are either admired or ridiculed.

Do you know anyone like Ike? Or are you unique like him? What makes you stand out from a group of people - from your family members, peers, or colleagues? What differentiates you from others? What abilities, aptitudes, or physical characteristics set you apart from everyone else? What is your uniqueness, that distinctiveness that puts the spotlight on you?

These rare attributes are a part of you for a reason. Many times, your life purpose is hidden in your uniqueness. Your question then becomes, "Why was I born this way and what can I do or become as a result of this uniqueness?" The answers will guide you to discover your life purpose.

Your Uniqueness is Your Strength

Your uniqueness is your strength, wealth, and a blessing to be treasured and celebrated. Your rarity is your power, a key to your greatness and influence and it must be harnessed. Unfortunately, many respond to their differences like Ike did. They attempt to destroy or alter them, so as to blend in and become common and ordinary. However, your uniqueness makes you extraordinary.

Many great people in history were those who ignored the criticisms of others and went ahead to achieve greatness through their uniqueness. Many were mocked and ridiculed but they searched out their life purpose within their uniqueness and made a name for themselves in history.

It's through your uniqueness that you shine. By turning your uniqueness into strength and celebrating it, many critics will be won over, eventually. For instance, Khoudia Diop, also known as the Melanin Goddess, is a young Senegalese lady, who was ridiculed because she was distinct in her skin color. She was not just dark-complexioned, but charcoal-dark, and that separated her from many other Black people. As a result, she was ridiculed and, for many years, she suffered silently.

Later, instead of succumbing to her critics, Ms. Diop began to celebrate her complexion. She started posting pictures of herself on social media, despite the negative onslaughts they drew. Since she was created for a reason, she decided her unique skin color had a purpose and must be displayed. So, she started a career in modelling. There, her skin tone set her apart from other black models and, today, she is a successful model and actress.

Your uniqueness is your visibility. It gets you seen, heard, and announced. Without it, you remain invisible. But once you harness and celebrate your uniqueness, it will give you a platform to make a difference in the world. The beautiful Melanin Goddess now inspires young girls to embrace their looks, despite body-shaming critics.

For a long time, the fashion industry's definition of beauty has been skinny, size zero figures. As a result, while some women have nearly starved themselves to death in an attempt to qualify, others have felt stigmatized and ugly.

Thankfully, some women are now notably challenging the status quo and this definition of beauty. Regardless of their size, they've ventured into modelling because they realize that some women could never be a size zero, due to their bone structure – the way they were created. Therefore, their looks must be celebrated, as well.

The courage of these women to delve into their uniqueness and celebrate it has brought hope to many others. Your uniqueness is a special gift that must be accepted, celebrated, then developed. It must be magnified and announced and, when you do, it will make you successful.

There are some individuals whose purpose was hidden in their uniqueness. Let us look at some of them.

She Liked Vintage

Sophia Amoruso liked vintage fashion as a little girl. She hated the clothes her mum bought from the regular retail stores. She preferred old-fashioned clothes from decades ago. Her mum was perplexed; why wouldn't her daughter dress like her peers? Why did she opt for styles worn years ago, instead of trending ones?

Yet Sophia wouldn't succumb. Her mum would remain in the car, while she rummaged through old clothes in vintage stores. Unknown to both, this peculiarity would later make her a multi-millionaire.

At age 22, Sophia, who failed to complete her education, began to turn her uniqueness into a business. She started selling vintage clothes online. Her business grew as she put her personal twist on marketing and advertising her goods. She was passionate about her love for vintage fashion. Fast forward eight years and, at age thirty, Sophia had become a successful entrepreneur, whose company, Nasty Gal, was valued at 350 million USD.

Sophia discovered her purpose through her uniqueness. She may not have known it, but our peculiarities are important pointers towards who or what we were created to be and do. She accepted her distinctiveness and turned it into a profitable business, becoming a multi-millionaire in the process.

What are your peculiar passions or hobbies that people have tried to make you give up or change? Sometimes, your uniqueness may be a source of embarrassment and people may try to stop you. In Sophia's case, her mum tried unsuccessfully to dissuade her from wearing vintage clothes. But the important thing is to recognize your uniqueness and discover your purpose through it.

Unique Talents and Abilities

Uniqueness may be manifested in unique capabilities and talents. It's important to recognize that these abilities distinguish you from the masses for a reason. Some individuals with strange abilities assume careers in entertainment, leaving their audiences with eyes and mouth agape. I enjoy watching *America's Got Talent,* a TV talent hunt that highlights breath-taking talent exhibitions. There, you also see a lot of weird acts!

Purpose in Disabilities

Undoubtedly, we look different from each other, but certain people are unique, as a result of their disabilities. Although it may be disheartening, your purpose may be concealed in the aspects of yourself you struggle most with, since they differentiate you from everyone else. This isn't the most comforting news for someone dealing with a disability, but nonetheless, it's a possibility. Your purpose may be tied to your disabilities.

Seeking purpose in your disability could become a coping mechanism that draws your attention away from your pain to something positive and worthwhile. Rather than wallowing in self-pity, this paradigm shift could help you find meaning in your existence. When you ask, why am I unique? And how can I use this uniqueness to serve humanity? You're drawn into a cause higher and bigger than yourself.

There is a young man who searched for purpose in his disability; his name is Nicholas James Vujicic. Nick is a Serbian-Australian, who is popular all over the world, as a result of his deformity. Nick was born without limbs, no arms, or legs, due to a rare genetic disorder.

His mother initially refused to see him after his birth but eventually accepted his condition, believing there was a reason for it. Nick was bullied constantly, attempted suicide several times, but eventually came to terms with his disability. He chose to discover purpose through his uniqueness, since there were only seven known individuals suffering from the syndrome worldwide.

Nick turned his deformity into a platform to encourage people and today, he is a university graduate, motivational speaker, author, evangelist, husband, and father of four children. His disability has opened great doors of opportunity, not easily accessed by most people.

Nick has used these opportunities to touch lives all over the world. Many people are challenged to pursue their goals, irrespective of life's challenges, when they consider Nick's personal achievements, despite his struggles. "If Nick could face life without limbs, why should I give up because life has become very tough? If he could face bullies and become successful, why can't I?" they reason.

Helen Keller was another example of a person who discovered purpose in her physical disability. After a childhood illness left her blind and deaf at 19 months, Helen was shut up in complete darkness and silence. Later, she got an opportunity to live through the help of an instructor, who taught her sign language.

Despite being blind and deaf, Heller faced life head-on. She became the first deaf-blind person to earn a college degree. She looked within her disability to discover her purpose. She chose to become a role model to other deaf and blind people and used her opportunities to advocate for causes that were dear to her heart. She was an activist for women's suffrage, as well as other political issues in her day.

Despite her disabilities, Helen lived a life that inspires people to fulfill their purpose, despite physical limitations. If a blind-deaf woman could earn a college degree, author twelve books, become a lecturer, and a vocal activist, then no one has an excuse not to fulfill their goals. Keller received numerous awards and accolades during her lifetime and posthumously. In fact, the house where she was born in the US is now a museum.

Nick Vujicic and Helen Keller discovered their life purpose in their uniqueness - physical disabilities - and used it to touch lives around the world. Today, their stories give people a reason to live and overcome life challenges.

Purpose must be discovered in all your uniqueness. Whether you're different in your abilities, hobbies, tastes or as a result of disabilities, you're different for a reason. Your differences must first be accepted and celebrated to silence the critics, then developed to become a source of blessing and inspiration to others.

Money is good, isn't it? Now let's learn the role money plays in revealing your life purpose. Ready? Let's do it!

The Golden Nuggets

➢ Your uniqueness sets you apart from others.

➢ Your differences could be in your abilities, talents, hobbies, or physical attributes.

➢ You may be either mocked or praised for your distinctiveness.

➢ You must first accept your uniqueness, then celebrate it.

➢ Your differences must be developed to be a source of blessing to humanity.

➢ Your life purpose and fulfillment could be found in your uniqueness.

➢ Don't ever reject or trivialize your uniqueness – it makes you special!

Study Exercises

➢ What are your unique abilities, hobbies, or attributes?

➢ What differentiates you from family, friends, or peers?

➢ Do you have any disabilities?

➢ What are the differences that have attracted praise, criticisms, or ridicule from others?

➢ Compare your list of unique attributes to your lists from previous chapters. Are there any recurring item(s)?

➢ Do you see any career possibilities connected to your uniqueness?

➢ How can you celebrate and develop your uniqueness to be a blessing to others and a source of income for yourself?

Chapter 10

Not for Money or Prestige

"Money isn't the most important thing in life, but it's reasonably close to oxygen on the 'gotta have it' scale." —Zig Ziglar.

Money is a great motivator. It influences most of our decisions. Often, people select a job or career, based on financial rewards. Others move from one state or country to another, in pursuit of bigger paychecks. In fact, some people select their spouses based on financial considerations. In certain situations, marriages are arranged to boost the financial status of both families. So, money is one of the greatest influences in our world.

Although money motivates, when it comes to discovering your life purpose, the opposite is a particularly important clue. Whatever you're willing to do, irrespective of financial rewards, is a clue to your life purpose. This means that money isn't a factor, just pure, unadulterated passion. Your purpose is tied to passions that eclipse financial rewards.

What would you do, even if there were no guarantee of financial reward? Would you still want to be an actor, doctor, musician, or pilot, if there were little or no monetary gains involved? What would you do for free? What would you do sacrificially? And if you're currently working, would you continue in that job, even if you received one million dollars overnight or would you quit in a jiffy?

Money is indeed a great motivator. However, for anyone who has discovered their purpose, the allure of money isn't powerful enough to distract them. What are you motivated to do that money cannot lure you from? Tough question, huh? If you can identify it, then you have discovered your life purpose.

I heard of a high school chemistry teacher, who wouldn't be tempted from his purpose. Greg (not his real name) won the lottery and became a millionaire overnight. When asked his plans, Greg replied that he would go on vacation for two weeks, then return to his classroom. He explained that he couldn't imagine a life not teaching high school chemistry!

Money was not a motivator to Greg, teaching chemistry was. It's obvious that Greg had discovered his purpose. That's because whatever motivates you more than money is your life purpose.

Purpose is not for Money

"Don't concern yourself with the money. Be of service... build...work...dream...create! Do this

and you'll find there is no limit to the prosperity
and abundance that will come to you."
—Earl Nightingale

Unfortunately, many people work purely for money. After a while, they get bored but since the money is good, they remain in the job, depressed on Mondays and excited on Fridays. There are certain things we do strictly for financial rewards. They may be opportunities to increase our streams of income. Those are commendable but must not be confused with your purpose. Purpose is found in those things you're willing to do, irrespective of financial incentives.

It's true that many countries are poor. They are in financial hardship, and their future is bleak. As a result of these uncertainties, some parents advise their children to go for careers that will guarantee them a decent future. These youngsters sacrifice their purpose on the altar of financial security. They allow fear of financial hardships to dictate their career paths. Fear should not be a motivator; rather, we must encourage young people to courageously pursue their purpose, irrespective of their fears and concerns.

"But how do I meet my financial obligations if money isn't my goal?"

Money always comes as a compensation, while fulfilling your purpose. Accomplishing your life purpose does not imply that you should be poor and broke. Rather, your life purpose is the area where you're rewarded both financially and emotionally. Money will always come when you're fulfilling your purpose. Therefore, allow money to be a compensation, rather than a motivation.

Why are you reading that course in college? Why are you in that business? Is it solely to make money? If so, then you've made a mistake, because money isn't supposed to be your main motivation. Anything you're doing just for financial gains isn't your purpose.

Dear teenager, looking forward to a great future, what do you want to do with your life and why? Why do you want that career? Is it because the salary is something to smile about? Wrong reason!

I met a young Indian girl recently at the coffee shop. She was reading a big textbook, in which I could see pictures of the human heart. I could tell she was in the medical field. Later, I struck up a conversation with her and she explained that she was a nursing student, about to graduate. I couldn't help but ask, "Why nursing?"

Her response made me smile, for it was certain that she had discovered her life purpose. "I love to help sick people, especially the older ones," she gushed. As she talked about her love for helping sick people, she quickly interjected, "But not babies; they're so little, I'm scared of handling them!"

Unlike this girl, who is pursuing a nursing career out of passion, I have met nurses who are in the profession solely for financial rewards.

Due to the high availability of nursing jobs plus the attractive pay package, many flock into the profession. But, without the passion for the role, nursing can be a difficult and demanding job that results in dissatisfaction and burnout. Financial gains should not be the determinant of your purpose and career. Your purpose is found in those things you're passionate about, irrespective of financial returns.

You ought to pursue a career that's connected to your purpose. You should select one that stirs your passion, your enthusiasm and fills your heart with joy. You should be doing whatever satisfies the deepest longing of your heart.

You must pursue whatever brings you inner satisfaction and fulfillment, as you help others and make life better for humanity. The longer you live, the more you'll realize that fulfillment isn't found in money but in doing the things for which you were created.

What Would You Do Sacrificially?

Another clue to determining your purpose is those things you would do sacrificially, going the extra mile and sometimes incurring personal loss or danger. Purpose is like a burden within you that's greater than personal needs or desires. It's a deep yearning to solve problems for humanity before considering your own needs. So, look inside, and ask yourself: is there anything you would do sacrificially?

Whatever you're willing to do sacrificially is a clue to your life purpose. This isn't quite common because the price is huge, and many are unwilling to sacrifice so much for others.

There are missionaries who have sacrificed their comfort, friends, and families to live in remote places around the globe. They expose themselves to danger, hunger, and diseases and some have lost their lives in the process. This type of work is only done by people who have identified it as their purpose.

Mother Teresa was known for the sacrificial life she lived. She was burdened by a desire to help the poor and sick. Although a teacher, a principal living comfortably, she gave that up and moved into a convent.

Later, she gave up even the comfort of the convent to go live with the needy in the poorest neighborhoods. It was a difficult move, and she was tempted to return to the comfort of the convent, but her faith and passion for the poor kept her going.

In addition to missionaries, there are some careers that are extremely dangerous and pose a significant risk to one's life. Kudos to people in careers such as firefighting and the military. They pledge their lives to safeguard their nation and defend its interests.

In the course of their job, some become maimed or lose their lives. These careers are motivated by sacrifice. So, whatever you're willing to do selflessly is a hint to your purpose.

Purpose is not for Prestige

Aside from financial gains, another reason people select a career is because of the prestige and respect attached to it. This may vary in diverse cultures, but most times, you find that careers such as medicine, law and engineering make the top of the list.

As a result, some select these top professions, regardless of their calling. But a clue to your purpose is that which you are passionate about, irrespective of its position on the 'prestige ladder.' Your purpose isn't a search for fame or respect but that which you were created and designed to do.

Within the Nigerian context, this pattern is quite common. Many parents expect their children to choose professions for financial and status reasons. They ignore their children's potential and push them into prestigious professions because they want to be addressed as *Mama doctor* or *Papa lawyer*. And when they gather for village meetings or parties, they proudly introduce themselves by their children's professions, instead of their names!

It's important to realize that no profession is superior or inferior to any other. There is dignity in all labor. You were created to do something important with your life, whether it's cleaning toilets or flying planes. The prestige and monetary status should not determine what you do. So, when you discover that which you're willing to do despite fame or glory, you've discovered your purpose.

I met a high school mate a few years ago in Dallas, Texas. She had matured into an incredibly beautiful lady and had also become a medical doctor. As our conversation bordered on career paths, she shocked me by announcing that her passion was to set up a janitorial business. "I love cleaning, especially toilets," she said.

Some years ago, a medical doctor in Nigeria gave up his prestigious career to pursue his passion – baking. He made headlines because this move was quite unusual. But the doctor-turned-baker ignored his critics and grew a successful bakery business.

These medical doctors discovered their life purpose and wouldn't trade it for prestige. Although they started out on the wrong foot, they were willing to alter their course and pursue their purpose. Whatever you're willing to do despite fame or prestige is a clue to your purpose. When it comes to life purpose, it's not about prestige but passion!

In my second year in pharmacy school, we learnt a new student had joined our class from the department of medicine & surgery. The news raised several eyebrows because, although some students had transferred to our class, her case was different. While others were supposedly stepping up the career ladder, Amanda was stepping down.

One year later, Amanda dropped another bombshell. This time around, she was leaving sciences for arts! Her passion was writing, and she had just published an anthology of poems.

She was intent on pursuing her passion. Our class organized a send-forth meeting for her, and she relocated to the United States to pursue her studies in Communications.

Years later, Amanda has become a household name, beyond the literary world. She has received numerous awards for her books and many honorary degrees from universities around the world. Her pursuit of purpose has given her both financial rewards and prestige that eclipsed her earlier career choices. What if she hadn't courageously pursued her purpose, our world would've been deprived of the outstanding literary works of Chimamanda Ngozi Adichie!

Purpose first, money follows. So, disregard money or fame and go for your purpose, for within are the seeds of greatness. Encapsulated in your purpose are the seeds of financial abundance, fame, and prestige. Don't make money or prestige your priority, make purpose your priority. Whatever motivates you more than money or fame is a clue to your life purpose.

Two heads are better than one, they say. Now, let's see how several heads can assist in unravelling your life purpose. C'mon, let's go!

The Golden Nuggets

➢ Your purpose is found in whatever motivates you more than money or prestige.

➢ Money should be a compensation, not a motivation.

➢ That which you are prepared to do sacrificially is also a pointer towards your purpose.

➢ Disregard the prestige ladder and seek your purpose.

➢ Purpose first, money follows.

Study Exercises

- ➤ What motivates you more than money?
- ➤ If you won the lottery, what would you still want to do?
- ➤ If money and prestige were not a factor, what would you be doing?
- ➤ What would you do sacrificially?
- ➤ Where would you want to serve humanity, despite inherent dangers?
- ➤ Compare your list with the lists from previous chapters. What items are recurring?

Chapter 11

What Do People See in You?

"If two heads are better than one, then three would make a difference." —Unknown.

Have you identified your life purpose yet? If yes, congratulations! But if you're unsure, don't worry because, in this chapter, you're going to learn another clue to discovering your purpose. However, unlike the others, this clue is about looking at yourself through the eyes of other people.

Here, you'll enlist the help of people who have known you for a long time, from childhood. These may include your family, friends, classmates, and teachers. We are going to analyze what they see in you that you're unaware of. Remember, two heads are better than one.

Two are Better than One

You're reading this book because someone saw in me what I couldn't see in myself. In fact, not just one person but several people, yet it was difficult for me to believe them. I loved reading and I wished I could write but I never considered it within the scope of my possibilities.

But I liked pen and paper and would often write down my thoughts. I drafted poems and short stories, and my readers enjoyed them and requested for more. "No, I'm not a writer, I don't have the talent," were my regular excuses. But the ability was there, in seed form, waiting to be harnessed. Unfortunately, while others could see it, I was blind to it.

Despite the encouragement and constant prodding from my sister, some friends, and a few classmates, I didn't change my views. But finally, when a mentor commended my work, I decided to believe them and give writing a try. Now, after six books as a ghost writer, with some monetary reward, I'm still like, huh?

There are potential people see in us, which we don't see. I'm remarkably good at seeing potential in people, yet I was blind to my own. That's because we're prone to put ourselves down and downplay our abilities. Has anyone complimented you on something, but you shrugged it off, claiming it was nothing to write home about? Due to this tendency, we're going to analyze your abilities through the eyes of others.

What Abilities do Others Compliment You on?

We have certain abilities that draw the admiration of others and, oftentimes, they praise us for them. We either accept their compliments or reject them due to self-doubt. Sometimes, we wonder if we're being flattered. But if these compliments are from different people and have been consistent for a long time, then maybe they are telling the truth. Those compliments may hold a clue to your purpose.

What compliments have you received consistently? You may have to travel back down memory lane to when you were younger. Why did people praise you? If you cannot remember, ask your family members. This is where you enlist their help. Is there something they often celebrated you for? What was it?

Like I said earlier, we have self-doubt. We have a little voice in our heads, telling us, "No, you can't do that." As a result, we limit ourselves and our possibilities. Then another person sees us. They see the potential and possibilities and compliment us. We need to pay more attention to them. Why? Because they don't hear the voices in our heads.

So, it's possible to get honest feedback on our potentials and capabilities from external eyes. However, this does not mean that everyone can see your potential. More often, the reverse is the case. There are sad scenarios where people have downplayed other's potentials and ruined their destiny. In this situation, however, we're looking at compliments that have spanned years and have come from multiple quarters.

A young man I choose to call Fred discovered his purpose because a friend saw his true potential. In his case, his family did not see this potential, as a result of their stereotypical mindset, but his friend did. I was that friend.

Fred had graduated from university and was seeking a corporate job. He applied to many companies and waited for an interview, but none was forthcoming. Weeks crept into months and, two years later, he was still job-hunting.

Fred was my classmate's older brother and I'd been close to the entire family for several years. So, when I visited during my vacation and realized that Fred was still living at home, job-hunting, I advised him to start his own business. I saw an entrepreneurial ability in him and encouraged him to try it.

My suggestion gave Fred the confidence to admit his dreams. He revealed that he was passionate about starting a business, but his parents wouldn't support the idea. They expected him to follow the family tradition by getting a white-collar job. After our conversation, Fred was encouraged, and he started a business.

Six months later, I visited, and Fred proudly showed me the small, used car he'd bought – his first car. His business was flourishing, and he shared his expansion plans with me. Two years later, when I visited the family again, Fred was living in his own apartment; his business had diversified, and he had some foreign partners!

Another strategy is to outrightly ask the significant people in your life what they think your purpose is. To make it easy and straightforward, write out the questions from previous chapters that resonate most with you and ask the people closest to you, whom you trust, to provide you with honest feedback. Write down their answers, then cross-check them with yours. If you see a consistent idea, that's what you're looking for.

What do People Envy You for?

Do people envy you? Now, I'm not referring to your cell phone, car, or designer wardrobe, but your talents and abilities. Unfortunately, in our imperfect world, people stoop so low as to envy others. We hate it, but today, we're going to get something positive out of people's envy. We will use their envy as a clue to discover your life purpose. How?

Usually, envy attacks your strengths and ignores your weaknesses. No one envies a broke, unsuccessful person. They may sympathize with them, but they certainly don't want to be in their shoes. People envy what they admire. Secretly, they may like you for it, but their insecurity prohibits them from acknowledging it. Oftentimes, self-confident people admire your strengths, while the insecure ones envy them.

Now, let's convert envy into a useful product. Envy attacks strengths, therefore, it reveals your personal strengths. Since purpose is usually tied to your strengths, voilà! People's envy could be a pointer to your life purpose!

We know how envy plays out, right? Rather than admit they like your talent, envious people will criticize you and say mean things. So, which of your abilities has attracted people's envy? Are you genuinely good at it? It's possible to overrate our talents, but if this ability attracts both compliments and criticisms, then write it down.

Having identified the strengths that provoke envy, you're going to subject them to the passion test. If your painting abilities are envied, are you passionate about painting? This determines whether painting should be considered as your life purpose. Lack of passion will rule out any strength, despite the envy or admiration it triggers. Remember that purpose must stir up deep emotions within you.

Based on these, you can discover your purpose through the eyes of other people, both admirers and critics. While the former praise and compliment your strengths, the latter envy them. Both reactions are valuable, because they can help you identify your strengths. And since purpose is usually connected to your strengths, they are pointers towards your life's purpose.

Before You Call it Quits

Still haven't figured it out? Don't give up. You need to read this book again. I guarantee that you'll find your purpose if you follow these steps faithfully. Remember that your purpose isn't a secret, and it's within you. Here are your next plans of action.

- ➤ Read the book all over again and, as you read it, have a pen and paper beside you.
- ➤ Write down any thoughts and ideas that flip across your mind as you read. Don't question or dismiss them, regardless of

how strange or impossible they might seem.

➤ I've asked a lot of questions besides those at the end of each chapter, so write down your answers to them as well.

➤ Don't over-think your answers. Write any and all answers that come to your mind.

➤ Then, at the end of each chapter, answer the study questions as honestly as you can.

➤ Review all your answers.

➤ What thoughts or ideas are consistent?

➤ What thoughts or ideas appear more frequently than others?

➤ If you can, narrow it down to two or three.

➤ Finally, invite a close friend or family member and run through the ideas with them.

➤ Focus on your final choice(s) as your life purpose.

The Golden Nuggets

➢ Your purpose could be discovered through the eyes of other people.

➢ While some admire and compliment your abilities, others criticize you, out of envy.

➢ Both the compliments and the criticisms are pointing towards your strengths.

➢ Your strengths are pointers towards your purpose.

➢ If you're unable to discover your purpose, read the book again and practice the exercises.

➢ Confirm your findings with close and influential people in your life.

➢ Your purpose isn't difficult to discover because it's right within you.

Chapter 12

What's Next?

*"The two most important days in your life are the
day you are born and the day you find out why."*
—Mark Twain

Congratulations for finding out why
you were born! Today calls for a
special celebration because you've
identified your life purpose. According to
American writer and lecturer Mark Twain, the
day you discover your purpose is as important
as your birthday, because that's the day you
understand why you were born.

Understanding purpose gives you a sense of
direction and focus. Now, you won't be distracted

by numerous options. And you can channel your time and energy like a laser beam towards achieving your purpose.

You may be wondering, what's next? That's going to be the subject of this chapter. You should not stop at discovering your purpose; you must take the next step to fulfill your purpose. So, come on, let's discuss the next steps, since you've discovered what you should do with your life.

Identify Related Careers

By way of recap, we learnt that purpose could be discovered through the following ways:

1. Your passions – what you love.
2. Your passions – what you hate.
3. Your natural talents.
4. Your temperament.
5. Your intelligence.
6. Your uniqueness.
7. What motivates you more than fame and money.

8. Through the eyes of other people.

With your purpose written down, the next step is to identify the careers or professions connected to it. Sometimes, your purpose is an obvious career, and this makes it easy for you. But if your purpose isn't a career, you'll have to conduct research on careers that are closely related to your purpose. Let's look at some scenarios.

Scenario one

You hate disorder passionately. There are several careers related to order, namely: law enforcement (police, bailiffs), legal careers (attorneys) or environmental order (urban developers and planners). Restoring order is an overly broad subject, therefore you need to bring other passions and strengths into consideration.

What are your passions? Assuming you love the outdoors, nature, greenery, then your focus should be environmental order. This will limit your search to careers related to bringing order and beauty to the environment.

What is your intelligence? If you are visual-spatial intelligent or picture smart, you may lean towards bringing order through architecture and urban development. But supposing you are nature smart, you may opt for preventing environmental damage, such as water or air pollution, etc.

So, you can combine your hate for disorder with your passion for nature and your intelligence type, to arrive at a career. This is a way to match your purpose clues to help you identify a career path.

Scenario two

You're an extrovert who loves animals with a passion. What careers relate to animals? Animal farming, veterinary medicine, animal grooming or training and so on. However, assume you keep an unusually high number of animals as pets, which people may consider strange or unique. Let's combine your uniqueness with your passion.

You may be looking at working at a pet boarding facility, to train, groom, and care for pets. Or you could work at an animal shelter to safeguard stranded animals and find them new homes. Your career choice must involve interactions with people, due to your temperament. In this way, you've used your uniqueness, passion, and temperament to arrive at a career choice.

Scenario three

You love children with a passion. What careers are connected to children? Teaching, caregiving, pediatric doctor, or nurse, etc. You are a Sanguine, so you have a temperament that would endear you to kids. You are also bodily-kinesthetic smart because you are good at sports; in fact, you are skilled at swimming.

A career opportunity may include being a swimming instructor for children. This will combine your passions, intelligence type and temperament. You may go on to have a swimming school in the future, as more opportunities open up to you.

Scenario four

When your purpose is a career in itself. For instance, you want to be an entrepreneur, or an engineer. But which area of entrepreneurship or engineering? This will be decided by your passions. Venture into the field that's related to your passions. If you love books and magazines, then a bookstore or book-related business will be ideal, instead of clothing. If you love teaching, then you may consider teaching engineering. Let your passions guide you.

These examples are far from exhaustive but, hopefully, you've seen how to connect your clues to arrive at a career that's related to your purpose. Hopefully, you've finally got your purpose and your career written down. Now, let's move on to the next step, which is to get educated.

Get Education

"If you think education is expensive, try ignorance."
—Derek Bok

The importance of education in achieving your purpose cannot be over-emphasized. You need to be educated in the area of your purpose. According to Derek Bok, American lawyer and former president of Harvard University, education is less expensive because ignorance will cost you much more, in the long term.

During the process of identifying your purpose, you analyzed your talents and abilities. Although you possess these gifts, you need to develop and sharpen them. Your natural abilities are not the end products. They are raw materials that must be processed to create the final product.

Never think of your talents as final marketable products; they are the crude version of the final product. Your strengths must be developed through education – either formal or informal. And you must exercise patience till they are fully developed.

Formal or Informal Education

You need quality education to be among the best in your field. Your education may be formal or informal. For some careers, I don't need to stress the importance of education because you cannot be licensed to practice, unless you've been to school. These careers require formal education. So, if your purpose is to be an architect, nurse, accountant, and so on, you need a formal university education.

But if your purpose is to be a chef, beautician, dress maker (some countries don't require licensing), getting a good education will still give you an edge over others. There are culinary schools where you can learn the best skills in cooking and also managing your culinary business. Education will widen your horizons and connect you to peers and instructors, who will help and challenge you.

If you're pursuing a career in music, there are music schools that will hone your talents. If these are available, enroll. Always remember that the best investments are the ones spent on yourself. As Benjamin Franklin said, an investment in knowledge pays the best interest.

Informal Education

Some professions require informal education. This means that you don't have to go to college to develop your skills. You may learn directly from someone in the field, a more experienced and successful person. This is called apprenticeship. This instructor will teach you the ropes about the career as you get practical, hands-on training.

You must determine your educational needs, either formal, informal or a mix of both.

Self-Education

In addition to the established educational requirements of your proposed career, you must not forget the education you acquire by yourself. This could be obtained through reading books, magazines, newsletters, attending seminars, researching online. You must continually sharpen your skills to remain abreast of the advances in your field.

Education never ends; even after graduating, you must continue to educate yourself. Jim Rohn, American entrepreneur, and motivational speaker, captures it succinctly: *"Formal education will make you a living, self-education will make you a fortune."*

Work Hard

One of my favorite quotes says: *"Hard work beats talent when talent fails to work hard."* Tim Notke

Talent alone won't get the job done. The importance of hard work cannot be over-emphasized if you want to be successful in your purpose. To achieve your purpose, you must learn not only to work hard but to love working hard. You must fall in love with work – smart, hard work. You must work so hard that everyone around you will attest to the fact that you're a hard worker. This is what brings success.

Many people are failures in life because of laziness. They prefer to watch TV, movies or indulge in social media, while their work is neglected. Doing so is a recipe for failure. You ought to devote your life to the fulfillment of your purpose. Your purpose must become your vision and there should be no distractions.

Make a personal decision that you'll become successful in life. Success does not depend on economy, race, gender, or family background, but on you. Since you're functioning within the area you were created and designed for, your success is certain if you, and only you, decide to make it so.

Don't let bad friends or unsupportive family members distract you. Let them know that you've discovered your purpose and you intend to make a success of it. Fall in love with work and with your purpose and you'll become a success. You asked a question, what do I do with my life? And here's your answer, use it to fulfill your purpose!

Preparation for Life Book Series

There are more skills you need to become successful in your purpose. However, they are beyond the scope of this book. This book is amongst others that make up the *Preparation for Life* series. I wrote them so a young adult could be better equipped to manage life. I advise you to get other titles from the series and become better prepared for life.

The Golden Nuggets

> The day you discover your purpose is as important as the day you were born.

> Your purpose clues will combine to help you arrive at the right career.

> Education is especially important for success in your purpose.

> Education could be formal or informal.

> Your natural abilities must be regarded as raw materials in their crude state.

> Your talents and abilities must be refined through education.

> People fail or produce mediocre results by using raw, undeveloped talents.

> Hard work is necessary for success in your purpose.

> Immerse yourself in your purpose and work extremely hard at it.

> Self-education is vital to stay on top of your career.

> Get other titles in the *Preparation for Life* series to equip yourself for success.

Study Exercises

➢ What were the purpose clues that helped you discover your purpose?

➢ Is your purpose a career or a profession?

➢ If not, how can you select a career using other purpose clues?

➢ What type of education does your purpose require?

➢ Are you willing to get educated or are your raw talents sufficient?

➢ How will you educate yourself?

➢ If you need informal education, have you identified a suitable mentor for apprenticeship?

➢ What will it cost you to achieve success in your purpose? Are you willing to pay the price of hard work?

➢ I hope we'll meet again in one of the books from the *Preparation for Life* series.

References

1. https://winkgo.com/top-65-monday-memes/ Top 65 Monday Memes to Help You Make It Through the Day

2. Jim Harter. July 29, 2021. U.S. Employee Engagement Data Hold Steady in First Half of 2021. https://www.gallup.com/workplace/352949/employee-engagement-holds-steady-first-half-2021.aspx

3. https://www.nimh.nih.gov/health/statistics/suicide.shtml

4. Front cover © Freepik premium stock